HOW TO BE A WINNER

HOW TO BE A WINNER

A Step-By-Step Guide to a Satisfying and Successful Life

NICK THORNELY
&
DAN LEES

HEINEMANN ASIA
S I N G A P O R E

Published by
Heinemann Asia, a Division of
Reed International (Singapore) Pte Ltd
Consumer/Education Books
37 Jalan Pemimpin, #07-04/05, Block B
Union Industrial Building
Singapore 2057

OXFORD LONDON EDINBURGH MELBOURNE SYDNEY
AUCKLAND MADRID ATHENS IBADAN NAIROBI
GABORONE HARARE KINGSTON PORTSMOUTH (NH)

ISBN 9971-64-323-5

Originally published in paperback by
Mercury Books
Gold Arrow Publications Ltd
862 Garratt Lane
London SW17 ONB

First published 1991
This edition 1993

Cover by Sam & Matt Design
Cartoons by Adam Preston

Printed in Singapore by Chong Moh Offset Printing Pte Ltd

CONTENTS

Whoever said there had to be losers?

FOREWORD

This book may well help you to become a millionaire but mere money-making isn't what being a winner is all about.

Real winners not only manage to achieve material success – without turning into complete bastards along the way – but also lead satisfying and fulfilling lives at home, at leisure and in the workplace. In fact, there are so many victories to be won, both large and small, that anyone can and should be a winner and can win without making other people feel like losers.

Mind you, there's an old Yorkshire saying that goes 'them as can, do – them as can't, teach', so are we ourselves winners?

We think so. We have always managed to provide ourselves and our families with warmth, shelter, food and usually a bottle of wine. We have had some professional success and have frequently managed to enjoy our work to the point where the word was hardly appropriate.

In fact, we and our families are almost indecently happy – we spend a lot of time touching wood – and certainly think of ourselves as winners, so much so that we regard things like serious illness or financial problems as minor interruptions in a lifelong winning streak. Winning of this sort is contagious. Winning becomes a habit and winners create and motivate winning teams wherever they may be and whatever the scale of their operations.

Like we said, this book may well help you to become a millionaire – in which case every other win you achieve will be a bonus.

Nick Thornely and Dan Lees

ACKNOWLEDGEMENTS

Ann Thornely, Sam and Lucinda.

Jeffrey Archer, Dan Asterley, Mike Baker, Chris Bayliss, Ken Bradford, John Bradley, Robin Breet, Tony Bryan, Chris Capron, John Chambers, Rt. Hon. John Cope M.P., David Cox, John Critchley, John Crook, Ken Dutson, John Davies, John Ford, Henry Foster, Peter Granzow, Richard Halsall, George Henderson, Lindsey Henniker-Heaton, John Hollingdale, Cyril Hollingworth, Sir John Hoskyns, John Knox, Dorothy Lees, Steve Lees, Ray Lewis, Iain Lindsay, Jimmy Lowe, Peter Lutman, Michael Maberley, Richard Marriott, Geoffrey Marshall, Richard Masterman, Muir Moffatt, David Monks, Bob Montgomery, John Neill, Simon and Celia Preston, Peter Robinson, Judy Sibley, Anita Sinclair, Derek Sturgess, Anthony Thornely, Ruth Thornely, Kay Weller, Martyn Wylie, Vivian Yuill.

1

ANYONE CAN BE A WINNER

Most of us want to be winners – which isn't too surprising as winners tend to be happier, sexier and more exciting than other people and, while they may or may not be richer, their lives have a champagne sparkle losers can never experience.

Take a look, for example, at the joy on the face of the racing motorist who has roared past the chequered flag to become a champion. As he sprays the applauding spectators with bubbly he may take a swig from the magnum – but he doesn't need it. He's already drunk with triumph and the realisation that his win will not only bring him increased fame and money but will enable him to take his pick of the best that life has to offer.

You can see the same joy on the faces of other obvious winners, like the tycoon who has completed a multi-million dollar deal or the actress who has won a coveted role, as they too celebrate their achievements in champagne to accentuate the bubbly, ebullient feeling that winning brings in its train, along with the tireless energy that enables winners to dance the night away while losers slink off home to lick their wounds.

No wonder most of us want to be winners and to put the sparkle into our lives that winning brings. The good news is that, while we may not all make the grade as racing drivers, film stars or tycoons, there is nothing to stop us becomin winners.

A WIN IS A WIN IS A WIN

The trouble is that most of us have been conditioned t regard life as a race or contest in which there can be only few winners, along with one or two runners up, while th rest of us remain sad and unlucky losers.

In many ways this conditioning is the fault of the medi whose constant focussing on the glamorous BIG winner persuades many of us that we will never be able to compete let alone win, and that our lot in life is to sit enviously o the side lines.

This, of course, is nonsense and, if winning were con fined to the small group whose triumphs receive nationa or international acclaim, life for most of us would b intolerable. The fact is that *anyone* can be a winner – th scale doesn't matter all that much, and the schoolboy wh finds a pound coin in his path probably feels more triumph than the multi-millionaire who wins a thousand pounds a the gambling tables.

If we are going to be winners, we have to fight hard against this media inspired conviction that winners are rarities or that there can be 'only one winner'. Watch the players in the next football match you see and you'll have no difficulty in identifying at least eleven winners when the victorious team does its lap of honour, not to mention the winning manager, the winning trainer and the rest, together with their thousands of 'victorious' fans.

Nor does the match have to be a championship game; you only have to think back to your school days to remember the joy of being a member of the school team – or merely belonging to the winning school.

People were experiencing triumph long before there was television or newspapers and long before winning became the apparent prerogative of the rich and famous. Primitive tribesmen, for example, who returned home from the hunt with enough meat to feed their families, were winners in a very real sense and their achievements were duly celebrated by the whole tribe.

Today we call people who come home with the wherewithal to feed their families 'breadwinners' and while, for some reason, a disparaging element has crept into the phrase – perhaps because breadwinners are not regarded as being particularly glamorous – they are *winners* and it's perhaps time both they and their families recognised the fact.

PRIZES FOR ALL

Life is not a race, even though the analogy is a seductive one and may occasionally be useful. In fact, life isn't a sporting contest of any sort, which is just as well since a life with only one winner and only one prize would leave nothing much to live for for the rest of us.

Fortunately, in every life – and especially in every working life – there are thousands of prizes to be won, which means that everyone can be a winner and that there are prizes for all of us whether we are bosses or office boys, factory floor workers, secretaries, sales staff or foremen.

The great thing is that to be a winner in the game of life – as opposed to artificial contests, sporting or otherwise – you rarely have to beat any other person in the sense of

Anyone can be a winner

making them look and feel like losers. In fact, in order to begin winning the only person you have to beat is *yourself*.

For life's real winners, winning works out much more like a bargain than a battle, with all parties feeling they have gained. In other words, everyone finishes up a winner.

NOTHING SUCCEEDS LIKE SUCCESS

There was once a newspaper editor who advised journalists to 'avoid clichés like the plague', which was perhaps his way of acknowledging that clichés often embody more wisdom than appears to be the case.

For instance, there is a lot of truth in the cliché that 'nothing succeeds like success' because being a winner is very much an attitude of mind and one which can be cultivated. As we'll see, winning is a habit and to win even one of life's *minor* prizes puts you in the running for more and bigger victories.

Getting the winning habit can put a champagne sparkle into our lives that will last for ever, rather than fading away as it may do after a once in a lifetime victory, but acquiring the winning habit may involve a rethink when it comes to identifying our goals.

IDENTIFYING GOALS

Identifying long term goals is a useful exercise and even a little day-dreaming about them can be fun. However, to be obsessed with major goals to the exclusion of everything else can be a recipe for unhappiness, because if you don't achieve your ambition when you feel you should, you are going to be miserable. You'll also *worry* and, when it comes to winning, worry is counter-productive.

It's much more satisfying – once you've identified your main goal and spent a little time dreaming about how great it would feel to achieve it – to set yourself a number, in fact the largest possible number, of interim targets, the achievement of each one of which counts as a win.

Don't forget, if you do it this way you will have enjoyed any number of victories in the course of pursuing your final goal and, while this will make you much more likely to win through than would otherwise be the case, should you by any chance not win your final goal – say, through circumstances beyond your control – you won't feel anything like as miserable.

A NEW FORMULA FOR SUCCESS

Most people would agree that, on the whole, **Winners are happy – Losers are miserable** which means – if you accept the conventional idea of a winner as the lone, laurel wreathed victor – a great many of us are condemned to spend our lives in misery, especially at work. After all, there are always going to be more workers than managing directors and more typists than office managers.

However, if we turn the formula round and say **Happy people are winners – Miserable people are losers** we get a whole new perspective on winning because in any given work situation there can be any number of happy people and therefore any number of winners – it's up to us to make sure we are among them.

WHY DO WE WANT TO WIN?

In case anyone thinks that all we have been doing so far is playing around with words, we can now ask ourselves why we want to win and what there is about winning which is going to make us happier? In other words, what are the incentives, provided by ourselves or by others, which will persuade us to aim for a specific goal, the achieving of which we will consider as 'winning'.

MONEY ISN'T EVERYTHING

People who say 'Money isn't everything' usually have enough of the stuff – and are generally talking to people who haven't – so it's not surprising that the phrase is regarded with suspicion, not to say cynicism. However, there is no reason why the idea that there are other sources of satisfaction than money, especially at work, should be rejected out of hand.

Money, of course, can be useful to gratify many of our desires and to provide many different sorts of satisfaction so there's no denying that in the workplace it is a major incentive, if not *the* incentive. It's also a useful measure – although certainly not the only measure – of attainment.

This being the case, employers who offer non-financial incentives *instead* of money can hardly be surprised if their proposals are greeted with suspicion. On the other hand, those who offer non-financial incentives *in addition* to a fair rate for the job stand a very good chance of employing potential winners and thus becoming winners themselves.

We'll be returning to the subject of money later – in almost any work context it would be unrealistic not to do so – but for the moment let's accept, if we can, that there are other forms of incentive, other ways in which we ourselves, as well as other people, can persuade us to become winners.

IF NOT MONEY – WHAT?

One of the easiest ways to discover if there are non-financial incentives which would persuade us to strive for any particular goal and to make ourselves winners, is to imagine that we already have all the money in the world, or at least more than enough for our needs. Okay, we might loaf around for a while, maybe even for months, but eventually most of us would begin to crave some form of activity and even if we were to tackle something which, on the face of it, wasn't work – like taking up golf or tennis – we would find ourselves trying to improve our game – trying, in other words, to become winners. In fact, people who become multi-millionaires often do go on working, and working very hard, even though it is difficult to believe that they need more millions or yet another private jet.

PRACTICAL WINNING

So, you have a million or two – what would be *your* incentives? Our list is opposite and we'll be looking at some of them in detail later. Perhaps you can add a few of your own.

Do not be surprised if your list is a short one, as it may mean you are reasonably content with your lifestyle. Getting more from what you already have is a certain way to feel more like a winner.

WHEN YOU HAVE YOUR MILLIONS WHAT WOULD YOU DO?

List	Ideas
PERSONAL SATISFACTION	Learning to paint watercolour landscapes
A SENSE OF ACHIEVEMENT	Reducing your golf handicap to single figures
CHALLENGE	Climbing the Andes
SOCIAL ADVANCEMENT	Attending a Garden Party at Buckingham Palace
POWER	Going into Politics
COMMUNITY SPIRIT	Raising money for charity eg National Trust
STATUS	Owning the biggest swimming pool in your area
SOCIAL CONSCIENCE	Donating money to those less fortunate than yourself
PATRIOTISM	Organising a challenge for the America's Cup
BUILDING SOMETHING FOR THE FUTURE	Funding a museum
PRESTIGE	Becoming chairman of something

Even from this short list it is obvious that there are many forms of incentive besides the financial and also that many of them are interlinked; several factors, for instance, combine to produce personal satisfaction.

DOWN WITH WORK

Incentives and final goals are well worth thinking about. And perhaps we should take a long hard look at the attitude that work is somehow a good thing in its own right.

It's worth examining, too, statements like 'Hard work never hurt anyone'. Rubbish! Hard work, whether physical labour or stressful mental work, can kill people. 'Work ennobles' is another pronouncement in a similar vein. Try telling that to Third World kids who labour in sweat shops. The Germans have the right idea about this one. They say 'If work ennobles, I'll stay a commoner'.

It's also said that if work were really the great thing it's cracked up to be the rich would have kept it for themselves! Certainly 'working class' would never be used in a disparaging way, as it often is. In other words, work – in the words of the old joke – is 'the curse of the drinking classes' so perhaps we should avoid it at all costs.

We have to admit that a book designed to show people *How to be a Winner*, especially in the workplace and which begins by advising people to work as little as possible needs a bit of explaining. The fact is that we firmly believe that in many cases *work is an activity undertaken reluctantly and which is fundamentally unpleasant*.

If you think about it, it is obvious that some work is enjoyable while other work is not:–

Working for subsistence pay: Working to live, especially if the work is unpleasant, can be regarded as genuine work.

Working for 'good money': This is a grey area as far as work is concerned; already an element of 'play' is creeping in as we are working for pleasant things, like houses, cars, good clothes and holidays. However, if we hate every minute of it, it is still work.

Working for good money when you enjoy some of what you do: This is where we begin to be *winners*. The more we enjoy the activity for which we ultimately receive money the less it deserves to be called 'work'.

Employment, whether on our own behalf or with others: The word 'employment' originally meant to implicate or involve, which is more of a winning approach. Of course, even in the best types of employment, we may find ourselves having to do some 'work' within the meaning of the Act.

It's a truism that not all jobs are the same and that some forms of employment offer more opportunity for enjoyment than others. However, *all* jobs provide some opportunity for gratification.

Even slaves probably derived some enjoyment from their work. They certainly enjoyed singing work songs and one can imagine a day when the skies were blue and the sun warm, when the work seemed almost a way of beating time to the music and life seemed pretty good, if only for a moment.

In fact, we could draw a graph with slavery at the bottom of the scale and total unadulterated enjoyment at the top, although the job that was all enjoyment would be pretty boring after a while.

Real winners get plenty of satisfaction out of their jobs – enough to allow them to enjoy going to work and to look forward to it – but at the same time they experience enough challenge to make the job interesting without being stressful.

LOSERS CAN BE WINNERS

Sociologists have identified a tendency to promote people above their real capabilities – a situation which can cause the person concerned a great deal of stress and unhappiness. This is a good example of an apparent winner who is, nevertheless, a loser.

If apparent winners can really be losers then apparent losers can be winners and in the situation mentioned above, for example, if there were two candidates for promotion, both equal in every respect, and one was promoted beyond his level of competence, then the candidate who missed out on promotion would be the real winner.

In other words, **apparent losers can be winners, apparent winners can be losers.**

WORKING TO WIN

As we have noted, hard graft isn't always 'work' and you can keep busy at your job and still enjoy it! Of course, in order to be a winning situation, this sort of job should also be reasonably well paid. *Job satisfaction is a bonus.*

However, there are cases in which no money is involved and in which the effort required, over long periods of time, is enormous. A classic case is the Marathon for which thousands of men and women train hard for months and then run 26 miles, 385 yards, most with no intention of achieving personal financial gain. All the runners who complete the course – and most of those who don't – are regarded and regard themselves as 'winners' and derive enormous satisfaction merely from taking part. They would certainly not see the immense effort they put in as being work unwillingly undertaken.

Once we discover what motivates people to make this tremendous effort, we will be able to use this form of motivation, together with all the other forms of non-financial incentives, to help us become winners.

WINNING IS CONTAGIOUS

As we've seen, winning is a habit, but it is also contagious. Join a winning team, even as an also ran, and you stand a very good chance of becoming a winner yourself.

What we are seeking is the sort of *super-incentive* that in wartime persuades perfectly ordinary people to make tremendous sacrifices, put in colossal effort and take horrendous chances, up to and including risking their lives. We need to generate the sort of excitement which in wartime makes people claim that they have never felt so alive – but of course we need to do so in peace time.

We need that champagne feeling in our lives, especially our working lives, that comes from being a winner.

WINNING IS SEXY

Winners are sexy – motor racing champions, for example, are usually surrounded by bevies of beautiful girls and even homely winners like Henry Kissinger always seem to have attractive women at their side. And nowadays, female winners are sexy too.

In fact, there is a definite correlation between winning

and sex – presumably with evolutionary importance. Perhaps for this reason, winning itself is sexy and winning at work, for example, can produce feelings akin to sexual gratification. Not everyone who goes to work knows this.

WINNERS AND WINNING

Obviously, winning and losing are not always the straightforward issues they appear to be.

As we've stressed, *everyone can be a winner*, but what constitutes a winner, how do you recognise a winner and, most important of all, how can *we* become winners?

Tips from the Top

Martyn Wylie, Managing Director of Colt International, runs a 'winning organisation'. Here are his six golden rules that he gives to every new recruit at Colt:

1. Do more than just get by.
2. Train and be trained.
3. Take advantage of every opportunity.
4. Be fair to the company.
5. Seek solutions and not problems.
6. Enjoy your work – and smile.

2

WHAT MAKES A WINNER?

Playing 'Spot the Winner' is easy – after all winners do tend to stand out from the crowd – but deciding what makes them winners and how we identify them isn't quite so simple.

One thing that complicates matters is that being one of life's winners or losers is a matter of degree so that we need to judge our own place and that of others on a scale of, say, one to ten, or draw a simple graph with total losers at the bottom and super-winners at the top. What we are aiming for is a position as close to the top of our winning scale as possible.

At this stage it might be useful to estimate your own point on the winners' scale. Just how much of a winner or a loser do you think you are? Then ask a friend to estimate your position.

Don't lose sight of the fact that we are asking you to estimate your place on the graph *at the moment* because people, families, companies and even countries can change their position on the Winners' Scale dramatically.

Of course, if this were not the case there wouldn't be a lot of point in a book called *How to be a Winner*, but it is amazing how many losers believe that their place at the bottom of the scale is immutably fixed. Mind you, in the old days there were a lot of people around who were only too happy to assert that this was the case and even to maintain that 'winners' and 'losers' were ordained by God.

There are still a few such people around, but nowadays most of us realise that we can influence our place on the graph and the mere fact of reading this book is an acknowledgement of the possibility. *By accepting the possibility of winning you have taken an important step towards becoming a winner.*

Of course, although today there is no question of our place on any scale being fixed for ever, there are still people who enjoy more advantages than others, having been born, for example, beautiful or rich, and while occasionally too much wealth or too much beauty can turn people into losers, in general terms neither could be realistically considered a handicap.

Money, in fact, has never made people into automatic winners, but there was a time when whole sections of the population were divided into winners and losers on the basis of the particular stratum of society into which they were born.

THE CLASS SYSTEM – WINNERS AND LOSERS

The class system which attempts to divide people into classes ranging from lower class to upper class with any number of sub-divisions in between is still with us but, fortunately, it is no longer as constricting as it once was. In fact, it must be difficult for people who were born after World War II to imagine the class system as it was even between the wars, and TV Shows like 'Upstairs Downstairs' give only a vague idea of the real thing.

Today, many people find the terms 'upper class',

'working class' and so on objectionable but they are undeniably useful and, as the system effectively divided the whole population into *winners* and *losers* for centuries, it is worthwhile having a brief look at it to see how it operated and to find out what, if anything, we can learn from it.

The first thing we notice is that there were lower class winners just as there were upper class losers but they were considered rarities. In fact, there were probably a great deal more of both than was realised, but the interesting thing is that not only did the upper classes expect to be winners, but the lower classes almost without exception supported them in their expectations. Nor was this solely a question of wealth and position; a poor 'gentleman' – unless he was literally down at heel and often even then – would be usually treated with the utmost deference by members of the 'lower' classes.

GREAT EXPECTATIONS – AND WHY NOT?

The upper classes expected privileged treatment and almost always got it – which was quite a 'con' trick and one which worked for centuries. 'Confidence tricks' – in the criminal sense – are well named as they depend for much of their success on the *confidence of the perpetrator* and much the same applies in the social context. The upper classes received – and to a certain extent still do receive – privileged treatment, largely because they had been brought up to expect it.

Whole sections of society were trained to believe that they were 'winners' as of right, entitled to travel through life first-class and secure in the knowledge that even if they proved to be losers in some ways, they would lose within a supportive winning framework of family, friends, clubs, regiments and so on. Families and schools combined to encourage them in this comforting belief and provided a whole package of recognition signals like old school ties and accents which announced to all and sundry 'Here is one of life's winners'.

In the Services they were expected to become officers and usually did, in which case their winning expectations and recognition symbols were formalised. In the workplace, they expected to be selected as executive material and in many organisations they were considered the only possible choice for posts of any seniority.

Of course, it would be ridiculous to suggest that the class system has entirely disappeared, especially in Britain where it still flourishes – perhaps because the 'born' winners know they have a good thing going and are understandably reluctant to give it up. However, it is fair to say that the whole system is less stultifyingly rigid than it was and that now, more than ever before, *anyone can be a winner*.

UPPER CLASS TWITS – OR UPPER CLASS WINNERS

The upper classes have been winners for centuries so it does seem that they must have been doing something right. Of course, many of them, whatever they themselves may have believed, were never total winners because they allowed themselves to become smug, self-satisfied, arrogant and selfish in a way that real winners do not.

However, the majority – though few escaped smugness – were genuine winners so it is worth asking whether there are any win factors in their way of life which can be of use to anyone, whatever their class background, who wants to be a winner. Mind you, we are not advocating that we all turn into Upper Class Twits, but rather suggesting that when it comes to winning attributes like poise and confidence it's worth taking a look at the sort of people who have been poised and confident for centuries.

Once you have spotted a patently upper class winner or two, look out for a classless or lower class winner. It's surprising how many attributes and qualities they share. Whatever the background, for instance, winners are confident, well groomed and well dressed in the sense that they are totally comfortable in whatever they happen to be wearing. Winners attending formal dinners for example almost invariably look as though they were born wearing dinner jackets, but will still be readily identifiable as winners while wearing overalls or fishing gear.

'SPOT THE WINNER'

Although most winners look the part it is largely the winner's interactions with others that make him a winner, which means that winning is rarely a solitary occupation. In fact, winners are to be found almost everywhere and while it is important to be able to spot winners in the workplace, it is not always easy because their status as genuine winners can be obscured by hierarchical and other factors. For instance, it is a little difficult at first to identify a senior executive as a loser when he is surrounded by the trappings we have come to associate with winning, like a large office, a company car, secretary and so on. At the same time it may be equally difficult to spot, say, a typist as a winner who is poised, confident and happy.

This is why it's perhaps easier at first to spot winners in a social context where their winning status is not masked by position in the hierarchy. Try winner spotting in a crowded bar for example and you could well find that winners are served quickly without making a fuss while others who are shouting and brandishing notes or empty glasses are neglected. What's more they seem to be able to manage this whether the person behind the bar is a blonde beauty, an old crone or for that matter a retired all-in wrestler, simply because they have a winning presence. Of course, body language does come into it – winners don't hover uncertainly around the bar – but this is the natural consequence of their presence and their ability to project it.

Interestingly, the winner's ability to command good service is rarely resented by the other customers, even should he inadvertently be served 'out of turn', whereas they would have been furious had the same thing happened to a non-winner. This is the case not only in the social context, but in other environments including the workplace. In fact, it is worth noting that *real winners are rarely resented.*

Of course, being served reasonably quickly in a pub, while it may be desirable, is hardly vital but – as we shall see – *winning is habit forming* and a win in one area leads to wins in others. It's worth noting too that winners make getting good service appear effortless. Certainly they don't seem aware of having achieved anything remarkable because winning, in this sphere as in others, has become a habit.

Occasionally, even winners have to wait longer than they feel they should and this is where you will see winners shift gear, usually into the charm mode. 'A large gin and tonic please, when you have a moment' said firmly, but with a smile and without a hint of sarcasm, gives the essential information that the winner would like a drink, while 'please' makes it a polite request for help rather than an order and the 'when you have a moment' acknowledges that the person behind the bar is busy and at the same time establishes a suggestion of complicity.

The next thing to notice is that the winner anticipates a positive response; he expects to be served pleasantly and quickly and, as we have seen in the case of our 'upper class' winner, in total contradiction to what we may have been taught at school about 'not expecting too much', confident expectation puts the winner well on the way to a positive response. In fact, there are any number of maxims from our school days that need reappraisal, especially those designed to turn children into losers. Incidentally, winners frequently find themselves literally the 'centre of attention'; if there are three people in a bar, for instance, the one in the middle is often the winner in the group.

PRACTICAL WINNING

In a shop or pub try to become invisible – in some places this shouldn't prove too difficult. Attempt not to be noticed by the staff and see how long it is before someone asks if they can help you.

Next try projecting yourself as a winner using only body language. We don't at this juncture mean jumping onto the counter – although there's little doubt that this would work in emergencies – but merely looking as though you expect to be served. Positive posture, eye contact and a confident smile all help. So does movement – because as snipers and hunters know, movement draws attention.

Then try using body language together with a typical winner's phrase when asking for service.

As any hunter will tell you, movement draws attention

If you feel less than totally confident try using a tape recorder until you are satisfied you have hit the winning note before trying it out in a real life situation.

Use a tape recorder to practice winning in an imaginary situation in which two salespeople are chatting and seem oblivious to your presence. 'Good morning, I wonder if you could help me – I'm looking for a left-handed widget. Do you have one in pink?'

In seconds you have announced your presence in a pleasant fashion, stated your requirements, sought their help and neatly involved them in your quest. Record this several times until you are happy with it – then ask a friend or partner to help decide on your best effort.

This may sound contrived and manipulative, as will many examples of practical winning, but with practice a winning tone and a winning turn of phrase will become totally natural. *Winners do manipulate people but they do so without malice . . . it's all a question of habit.*

WINNERS DON'T CRAWL

Real winners don't go in for boot licking mainly because they 'know' they have no superiors – only people who are positioned above them in the hierarchy of the job, the office, the army or whatever. They treat people in authority with respect but one way to identify them is that they are easy in their dealings with their seniors.

Next time you are spotting winners in a social situation watch out for the after office hours gathering which includes the boss and identify the winner or winners among his subordinates. They will be the ones who are treating the boss with relaxed informality as 'first among equals'.

WHO ARE THE WINNERS?

In the workplace spotting winners is a vital function of senior management – often, but not always, themselves super-winners. We asked several genuine winners in top management how they spotted winners in their organisations:

Tips from the Top

Said **Cyril Hollingworth** who started working on a milk round at the age of 11, retired as a manager from Unigate aged 65 and has since started a new career with QED Industrial Motivation Limited at the age of 69, 'He or she always carry themselves well. Head up, shoulders back, walk purposefully, always as though they are going somewhere important every time. Always well turned out and appear confident even if they are not inside.'

Here's an example of a winner from **Sir John Hoskyns,** Director General of the Institute of Directors:

'Peter Utley was totally blind from the age of eight, but despite his disability became one of the most influential and brilliant writers and commentators. He absorbed an enormous amount of written material which was read to him, holding it in his mind and digesting it, and then producing beautifully written and flawlessly argued articles.'

Said **John Davies,** Managing Director of York Trailers:

'We are great believers in the virtues of positive thinking, and hold the conviction that enthusiasm and energy are the main attributes that anyone can offer a company. Academic qualifications here rank very much as a bonus and not a prerequisite.'

Example of a winner from **George Henderson,** Managing Director (Operations), Gallaher Tobacco:

'She pushed to become a high-reach fork lift truck driver – hitherto a male province – and has taken great pride in her work. With an "I'll show 'em" attitude, her truck is always clean and polished and she won "Fork Lift Driver of the Year Competition" at Wembley.

She takes pride in doing more than any other fork lift operator and is jolly and confident. She earns good money, and so does her husband, and her two children are doing well at school. She is very "happy in her skin" and a real winner.

"We are buying our own house, having holidays in Majorca, change our car every three years and my husband is horny as hell – what more can a girl want!"'

David Monks, Chief Executive of North Warwickshire Borough Council:

'Winners are very good at relaxing under pressure and when I'm interviewing candidates for jobs I always deliberately try to put them under pressure. Graham Hill, the Racing Driver, once said that he "concentrated hard on relaxing".

Winners have a presence, aura, charisma and feel confident. Perhaps it was because they were at peace with themselves because they had reached an optimum level of performance.'

John Neill, Group Chief Executive, Unipart Group of Companies:

'Winners are those who really take special care of their customers by providing outstanding personal service.'

'A winning boss is one who can operate his secretary's computer': **Anon.**

YOUR CHOICE

Now that we have had a chance to think about winners and losers we can make our own lists of winners and losers selected for example from Royalty, politicians, athletes, stage, film, TV personalities and so on, including fictional characters.

Is Her Majesty, the Queen, a winner for example? And what about Princess Margaret or Princess Anne? Remember that we are assessing winners on a scale of one to ten and that we are looking for total winners – not merely people with a great deal of power or money. Bear in mind, too, that anybody can move up or down the winning scale and that yesterday's loser may be today's winner. For example, we might place Princess Anne a great deal higher on the scale today than she was a few years ago, but what do you think? Next, assess your family, your friends and your colleagues, including the bosses, taking care to keep the lists in code or in a safe place.

Mind you, we have only begun to look at the question of *How to be a Winner* so keep all your lists and check them later on to see if your assessments have changed. Of course, the object of spotting winners at this stage is largely to pick up winning tips, which brings us back to practical winning.

PRACTICAL WINNERS

When it comes to clothes, taste is more important than money. A genuine winner can walk out of an Oxfam Shop looking as though he has spent a fortune while a loser can spend lots of money and still look like a tramp.

Money does help though and a good tailor for example won't normally sell you anything you don't look good in as he regards you quite properly as a walking advertisement.

Good tailors – or good dressmakers – don't come cheap so if money is a consideration aim for say three good basic outfits containing at least one extravagant feature like a silk tie or a designer shirt or blouse. Check out the prices of made to measure items: they are never cheap but you could be agreeably surprised and – as even winners have a childish side – you can get a lot of harmless fun out of leaving a cuff button 'accidentally' undone to show your suit is 'made to measure'.

Winners are usually able to pronounce foreign words – and for that matter English words – correctly. This is sometimes due to their background but more often than not to the fact that winners are self-confident and therefore not easily embarrassed, which means that they are never afraid to ask. It is worth checking, for example, if you are not certain of the pronunciation of frequently occurring words like Riesling (Reesling), Graves (Grahves), Rosé (Rosay) and Beaujolais (Bowsholay).

WINNERS AND 'FOLKS' PAS

Everyone, no matter how brilliant and sophisticated, is bound to put his or her foot in it every now and again. In fact, the only difference between winners and losers in this regard is that winners do not worry about faux pas, gaffes, solecisms or any other sort of booboo.

They prefer – as a matter of convenience – to be aware of such things as correct pronunciation and the conventions of polite behaviour but they lose no sleep over such trivia; self-confidence, humour and commonsense are all it takes.

PRACTICAL WINNING

Make your own lists of characteristics which apply to winners and those which seem more appropriate to losers. You could start with the ones we've been looking at and then add any that have occurred to you while Winner Spotting. You may for example have noticed that *winners are attractive people* or that *winners are rarely envious.* We'll be looking at these and other winning characteristics later so hang on to your lists and add to them as we consider how to acquire the winning habit.

Tip from the Top

'Dress for where you are going – and not where you've been.'

3

GETTING THE WINNING HABIT

As any gambler knows, being on a 'winning streak' is a magical experience, taking them into a world where they can do no wrong, where every card and every horse proves a winner, a world where the odds have no meaning and fortune favours the reckless.

Sportsmen too know the thrill of a winning streak, the rush of adrenalin and the iron-clad certainty that the vital serve will be an ace or the hazardous golf shot end up on the green.

Winners – real winners rather than lucky gamblers or on-form sportsmen – always appear to be on a winning streak; they almost invariably get the job or the promotion, often without seeming to try. We call such people 'lucky'; folk wisdom recognises their existence as 'jammy bastards' and soldiers refer to them with affectionate envy as 'Mars Bar Experts' implying that if they fell into the latrine they would surface clutching a well-wrapped chocolate bar.

WINNERS REALLY DO WIN

Winners really do seem to win more often than other people. It's almost as if they had a positive attraction for good fortune and, while a gambler's lucky streaks come and go, winners consistently achieve their aims in ways which make their wins appear inevitable.

Of course, there is no denying the existence of luck, even though some things like good health or affluence may well be the result of sound planning by the 'lucky' person's forbears.

However, this sort of inherited good fortune, while it may help give people a start, does not necessarily make them winners, any more than being dealt a reasonable hand ensures a win at cards. Conversely, being born without inherited advantages doesn't automatically condemn a person to be a loser.

In some cases, being born without 'advantages' can help make people winners by providing them with added incentives, although there is a danger that it may trigger off the sort of ruthless ambition which, while it may lead to material success, doesn't produce winners.

At the same time too many advantages can sometimes turn people into losers by making them idle, self-satisfied and inconsiderate. In fact, if you're ever tempted to envy people who were born with silver spoons in their mouths remember that some of them will never have the wit to find the bowl.

THE RICH MAN IN HIS CASTLE

Envying people who have been born with the sort of advantages we've been talking about is like envying the wind. It's the kind of envy that can give you ulcers, which is another reason why winners are rarely envious of anyone. It may seem unfair that some people get the chance to develop winning habits early on in life, but fortunately today almost anyone can become a winner.

There was a time, however, when God was thought to have decided in advance who was going to win and who to lose. In the words of the well known hymn, 'The rich man in his castle, the poor man at the gate. He made them high and lowly, and ordered their estate.'

What a load of Victorian codswallop! It was intended as an admonition to the poor to 'know their place' and a bit of Heavenly reassurance for the rich who at the time could still hear the echoes of the tumbril in every squeaky cart wheel and it's the sort of nonsense with which winners will have nothing to do whatsoever.

Of course, we know that the 'poor' man might have been passing the rich man's gate on his way home to a loving family or carrying one of the rich man's pheasants under his coat. For that matter he could have been waiting at the gate with a hired chaise in which to spirit away the rich man's daughter while the rich man skulked in his castle worried sick at the thought of losing his money, his gamebirds or his daughter.

If this were the case, the 'rich' man would be a loser while the 'poor' man would be a winner, so in this sense people's estates may well be 'ordered' in so far as their characters are predisposed towards happiness or misery. However, this is not governed by position or material possessions and – once the basics have been catered for – there are so many different ways of winning that life provides prizes for everyone.

By basics we mean food, warmth and shelter because without those it is tough – though by no means impossible – to even think of becoming a winner. Given the basics we can begin to consider the sort of prizes we wish to win, remembering that *what other people tell us will make us happy may not in fact do so* – so there is obviously more to this business of winning than meets the eye.

WHO WANTS TO BE A MILLIONAIRE?

Well, we do – to name just two – but, even so, there is a difference between us because, while one of us is serious about becoming a millionaire and has done a lot towards achieving his aim, the other is still jogging along happily in the confident expectation that, one of these days, it will start to rain money. Still, both of us consider ourselves to be winners – which brings us back to our definition of a winner as someone who is 'happy in his skin' and one of the secrets of attaining this sort of happiness is to get the winning habit.

As we've seen, people who have inherited wealth or position frequently become winners because they have been brought up to expect to win, which is all very well for them but what about the rest of us? Fortunately, *it is almost as easy to acquire winning habits as it is to pick up bad ones* and, by getting into the habit of winning, we can teach ourselves to expect success and how to project this expectation as a powerful positive force.

HOW DO THE 'LUCKY' ONES DO IT?

What the silver spoon merchants are able to do from an early age is to exert a degree of control over their own lives. Even exercising partial options in such matters as choice of school, choice of sport, holidays and so on means that most middle class children have some degree of control over their lives and that this increases rapidly as they get older so that, by the time they reach university, they have acquired the winning habits which will last them as long as they live.

Conversely, some of those who are less fortunate may well find that they have lost control of whole areas of their lives, in many cases without even being aware of it.

TAKING CONTROL OF YOUR LIFE

Taking control of our own lives is *the* most important step in the process of becoming a winner.

Of course, if you are dominated by bosses, subjugated by sales managers, crushed by customers, or even hen-pecked and harassed by your partner, the mere thought of taking control of your own life can sound ludicrous. How can you possibly take control of your own life if you are a typist with a dragon of an office manager, a secretary with a demanding and overbearing boss, a factory foreman with an autocratic works manager or a middle management executive with an M.D. who enjoys wielding the whip?

THE MOST IMPORTANT WIN

The answer is to take control of those parts of our lives which we *can* control, beginning with those which cannot be controlled directly by others.

In fact, although it may sound daft, *the most important victory many of us will ever win may be accomplished simply by getting out of bed.* Mind you, it does entail

It does entail getting out of bed a little earlier than usual

getting out of bed a little earlier than usual but even that doesn't sound much of a win. Its importance lies partly in the fact that it could well be our first triumph since deciding to become a winner and partly in what we can call the knock-on effect.

Say for example that, in order to get to work in time, we have to get up at 7.00 and that for several years we have been getting up at exactly that time because that is the very latest we can leave it – providing we rush our toilet, gobble down our breakfast and are lucky with whatever form of transport we use to get us to the workplace on time.

This means that – indirectly – our boss has begun to exercise control over us long before we even set off for work. In fact, it might just as well have been the boss's hand that set our alarm clock and the strident clamour of his bell that ordered us out of bed with the same imperious clamour as the old fashioned factory siren. The trouble is that, whether we realise this to be the case or not, we feel this control and resent it in a way which can poison the whole of our day.

However, the truth is that the boss can't exercise direct control over the time at which we get up. It is something which we control and – assuming that we don't wish to be late for work – our control can best be exercised by getting out of bed anything from a few minutes to an hour or so earlier than we have to. Getting up just ten minutes earlier, for instance, would allow time for a leisurely toilet, a civilised breakfast and a quiet stroll to the bus, or whatever, instead of a mad dash.

Instead of a mad dash

PRACTICAL WINNING

If you are one of those people who have timed the getting to work process to the nearest second, remind yourself of how it feels to get up feeling resentful and to rush through your toilet losing a few seconds here and there when you are unable to find a new tube of toothpaste or whatever. You know the feeling; you can't lay your hands on the shirt or blouse you want and this leads to a slanging match with your nearest and dearest which wastes more time and leaves only a moment for a snatched cup of coffee, most of which you spill. Because of all this you miss the bus or hit a traffic jam and arrive at work in a filthy temper which is not improved when you realise that your pay has been docked or that you are the target of some barbed managerial sarcasm. Even if nothing worse happens – and it usually will – your day is shot, and perhaps your evening too.

Now try imagining – you can do it for real later – that you have got out of bed just fifteen minutes earlier than usual, which gives you time to appreciate the fact that it is a beautiful day as you peer out of the window before taking a shower, getting dressed and having a leisurely breakfast. Naturally, as you are not in your usual tearing hurry, everything you need is to hand and you leave the house – perhaps after a few moments discussion of mutual plans for the evening – in good time to stroll down to the bus stop with a friendly greeting to any friends and neighbours you may meet on the way. If you are driving, you are early enough to take a slightly longer, less busy route than usual, arriving in comfortable time to find a parking place, check out the notice board and so on.

LOOKING FORWARD TO GETTING UP

Tough – but sometimes, a little change can make you look forward to getting up. Perhaps you are looking forward to trying a new toothpaste, a new shampoo, new bath soap, new deodorant, new lipstick, new hairspray.

Perhaps you are looking forward to wearing a new tie, new blouse, new underclothes, new belt. It is amazing how little things mean a lot. A win is a win is a win.

PRE PLANNING

Plan approximately what you are going to wear *the night before*. And check it.

Clean your shoes *the night before*.

To make you feel *really* good, wear a flower in your buttonhole or a spray for the ladies.

These little things cost *very little money*. You will enjoy buying them and look forward to using them.

WINNERS DON'T TRY TO SCORE POINTS OFF PEOPLE BY MAKING THEM FEEL LIKE LOSERS

Sadly, a situation which arises fairly frequently is one in which dominant personalities in executive positions devote a great deal of effort to scoring off other people, fondly imagining that by doing so they are proving that they are winners. They are, in fact, demonstrating that they are captaining a team of losers. Remember the old time Sergeant Major who told a squad of recruits 'I'm the boss and you are nothing' only to hear from the rear rank a muttered 'Some job – boss over nothing!' The aim of the genuine winner is to become a member of a winning team in a winning company, not a winner in a company full of losers.

Incidentally, on the subject of time and time-keeping, 'flexi-time' is a genuine winning concept in which everyone wins and nobody loses. It's great if your firm operates the system officially, but if not you can usually institute a personal version provided you can demonstrate to the boss that you are working the same hours or even fractionally longer than if you worked to a strict timetable.

TAKING CONTROL IN THE WORKPLACE

Starting the day as a winner is easy enough and, once you get to work, the way to win is to remain in control of your life. Of course, the amount of control you can exercise will vary according to the firm and your position.

However, some degree of control is available to everyone.

LET THE BOSS MAKE THE BIG DECISIONS

Remember the old yarn about the chap who told his mates at the pub that in his house it was always he who made the important decisions while his wife made the less vital ones. It turned out that he decided what their attitude would be on topics like arms control and international monetary policies while she decided where they were going to live, what car they should buy and so on.

Naturally, most of us have our own ideas about the way things are run in the company we work for but, while there are usually ways in a democratic society in which we can make our views felt, this is not normally a way in which we can become winners on a day to day basis. As we've seen we can begin to win by getting up a few minutes earlier than usual and, at the workplace, we can begin to win by taking control of our own lives in minor matters like the arrangement of the space in which we work.

If we work in an office for example, our desk and cabinets can be chaotic, cheerfully cluttered, efficiently tidy or obsessively neat. In most cases the choice – within limits – is ours but in the long run reasonable order and tidiness is going to make things easier for us and, as a spin-off, be more efficient for the company. In the first instance, we are concerned with the benefits to ourselves and this demonstrates a basic motivating factor in the process of becoming a winner, namely, *enlightened self-interest.*

SETTING INTERIM GOALS

When Michael Edwardes took over as boss of British Leyland, he discovered that more than 300 of his top managers were in the wrong jobs. This didn't mean that he thought they ought to have been running whelk stalls, but it did mean that he had to shift them to different positions within the company.

Finding exactly the right job for yourself is an ideal example of a major winning move, but to begin with it makes sense to consider some of our interim goals and those minor victories that are going to help us acquire the winning habit.

WINNING IN YOUR WORK AREA

Tidy your own patch, and don't let others mess it up.

Get yourself a good pen or pencil.

Get a good personal calculator if you need one.

Have your own notice board.

Put up your own calendar. The most decorative isn't usually the most effective. Get one to suit you.

Move tools, chairs, tables to suit you. Keep looking for small improvements.

Drink good quality tea or coffee. Experiment with new brands.

Footnote: However modest the purchase, it will always be appreciated.

PRACTICAL WINNING

Make a list, for example, of all the things – apart from murder – that would make life at work more pleasant, more enjoyable, less frustrating and more efficient than it is at the moment. These could include such things as getting a decent cup of coffee, obtaining a parking space, or submitting your expenses on time. However, if your list of possible wins includes getting the office grouch to smile it could be an idea to leave the list at home.

A GOOD DEED A DAY KEEPS LOSING AT BAY

We aren't suggesting that potential winners should get measured for haloes but merely thinking about what good deed you could do each day that could alter the way you think about the job and your colleagues. If, for example, you are a typist whose supervisor gets totally pissed off about one of your minor foibles, like leaving papers strewn over your desk when you go for lunch, try doing things their way for a change. If people *think* things are important they are important to them, which means you can make them feel like winners without too much effort or sacrifice. Real winners aren't usually calculating about such things, but, of course, casting bread on the waters is a good way of ensuring a supply of fish. If your subordinate has, for example, a wedding anniversary or for that matter a golf date, suggest they leave a few minutes early.

Blessed are the peacemakers but they do tend to get clobbered, so perhaps refraining from adding fuel to any fires that may be smouldering in the workplace should count as a good deed. People should feel happier and more like winners for having come into contact with you during the working day and this, of course, does you no harm at all.

No need to work after quitting time unless *you* want to – after all, you did get to work in good time. On the other hand there's no need to dash off and a good winning move is to join colleagues for a relaxing drink before setting off. It doesn't have to be alcoholic, especially if you are driving and it does give you a chance to avoid the worst of the traffic jams. This would mean that you arrive home after a winning day feeling like a real winner, which is not a bad way of ensuring that your evening will be a winner as well.

Tip from the Top

'It's tough being ahead of your time.'

4

STROKES FOR FOLKS

Like most animals, people love to be stroked, but unfortunately nowadays – especially in the context of the workplace – physical stroking could be misinterpreted, so in most cases we have to confine ourselves to verbal stroking and other less intimate gestures of appreciation.

Mind you, it does seem a shame that – in Britain at any rate – we have all but abandoned this useful form of communication, along with the rest of the contact gestures, so that we miss out on the genuine comfort of 'a shoulder to cry on' or the pleasant glow that we once derived from a real 'pat on the back'. People in other countries are much more demonstrative and to become a winner on an international scale you should at least be aware of the local customs in this respect, but as far as the British are concerned shaking hands seems to be one of the few contact gestures left to us.

For the moment, since the handshake is pretty much our only physical contact method of initial signalling, it pays to get it right. This should be absolutely self-evident but it is amazing how many people – especially men – condemn themselves as losers within the first seconds of meeting someone for the first time by using horror handshakes.

HORROR HANDSHAKES

Horror handshake number one is the macho maul or death grip, designed to leave the other person writhing in agony and often used by male executive losers to establish what they fondly imagine to be dominance. Some men habitually use this grip on women, presumably to demonstrate

Handshakes: 'The macho maul'

Handshakes: 'The limp lettuce'

which is the stronger sex, and although winners do not approve of violence as a rule, lady winners might find a high heel applied firmly to the offender's instep suitably discouraging.

Horror handshake number two is the limp lettuce effect, often combined with damp palms and totally self-defeating. This is sometimes made even more unpleasant by a total reluctance to let go, in which case it becomes the politician's linger. This is exceeded in unpleasantness only by the pseudo sexy handshake offered by some male executives to female subordinates, which is a really tacky abuse of authority.

PRACTICAL WINNING

Winning handshakes should be firm but gentle and should last not much more than a second. They were originally intended to show that you had no weapon in your right hand or concealed up your right sleeve. They should still convey much the same message today, which means that wet palms are out and that, for anyone who has naturally sweaty hands, surreptitious drying is in order.

Practise handshakes – they really are that important – first of all by shaking your own hand, then those of friends of both sexes. Do the whole bit, combining your handshake with a friendly smile and 'How do you do?' Imagine different scenarios for your handshake. Meeting your new boss for the first time, meeting new neighbours at a party, experiencing love at first sight in a splendid nightclub and so on.

Don't worry if you feel a bit silly at first. We wouldn't like to take bets on it but we wouldn't be surprised if more contracts, business and social, weren't won or lost on a first handshake, than because of any other single factor. *Winners create a good impression and your handshake can help you do just that.*

SEX IN THE WORKPLACE

Winners don't go in for 'sexy' handshakes, but both male and female winners use sex to help them win in the workplace and elsewhere. They'd be mugs if they didn't – and winners are not likely to neglect anything which could give them a winning edge.

This does *not* mean that winners are forever trying to 'score', especially in the workplace – far from it. It doesn't even mean that they 'come on strong', as our American friends have it, with every member of the opposite sex they meet. As we shall see, there is a correlation between winning and enjoying a successful love life, but for the most part, especially in the workplace, the winner is content to use sexual interaction on a low key level to attain such mundane advantages as a decent cup of coffee, access to a senior executive or a couple of minutes extra on the lunch break.

Winners use sex in this way almost without being aware that they are doing so and to a genuine winner, using the mysterious spark of sexual appraisal and approval, communicated in a glance or a subtle change of voice timbre, is all part of the stroking process. It makes the other person feel good; in fact it can make two people feel like real winners for the whole day – even though they may hardly have said much more to each other than 'Good Morning!'

WINNERS SEE PEOPLE

It is fairly easy to 'stroke' a person of the opposite sex by recognising their existence as a human being, especially if they are reasonably attractive, but sometimes it is not so easy with people of the same sex. Bosses – even very minor bosses – often drift into the habit of treating their subordinates as if they didn't exist as people.

By contrast, winners see everyone as a person and have a smile and a word for everyone, without, however, being so aggressively cheerful as to get on people's nerves.

A WINNING SMILE

Winners do tend to smile a lot – or people who smile tend to win a lot – so smiling is one winning habit to acquire as soon as possible. For one thing it helps you to feel a winner but, more importantly, it makes the people you meet feel like winners too. In fact, smiling is so important that some large organisations have run whole campaigns aimed at teaching their staff to smile.

This doesn't mean that winners should go around with inane grins on their faces – only that it's a good idea to greet people with a smile and to smile at fairly frequent intervals while you are talking to them. After a while, smiling becomes second nature, but because smiling is easy, don't knock it. It's an essential weapon in the winner's armoury.

In fact, being able to smile naturally is a real help when it comes to acquiring the natural good manners that all winners need. Of course, we are not talking here about the sort of 'manners' you might learn at a school of etiquette. A winner's good manners are considerate rather than formal

Winners smile a lot

so they can be acquired merely by taking a conscious decision to treat other people as you would wish to be treated yourself. 'Do as you would be done by!' doesn't apply only to children.

IT COSTS NOTHING TO BE POLITE

When it comes to winning, the magic words are 'please' and 'thank you' and the magic phrase is 'I wonder if you could help me'. For *practical winning* begin by using these words more often than before, especially in the workplace and in service situations like garages or shops. This may seem elementary, but so many of us are under such pressure in today's world that we respond by using a sort of verbal shorthand which cuts out all the grace notes like 'please' and 'thank you' which, though it may appear efficient at first sight, sounds like rank bad manners to others and could prevent us from becoming winners.

Saving one second by giving a brusque order rather than making a polite request is counter-productive, especially if the person concerned then spends several minutes complaining about your bad manners to a colleague. As for the magic phrase 'I wonder if you could help me?' few people can resist a request for help because it flatters them and gives them a chance to demonstrate their knowledge or expertise. Again, don't overdo it, but on the other hand don't struggle along without help that you need, just for the sake of asking. After all, the phrase 'Can you help me please?' has been known to work with Continental policemen so it can hardly fail in business or social situations.

PRACTICAL WINNING

How many times did you use the *magic words* today?

SELL YOURSELF – BUT SOFTLY

Winning, as we hope we are making clear, does have a great deal to do with selling ourselves and many of the attributes of the genuine winners are those we recognise in first class salesmen. In fact, there is no harm at all in reading a good book or two on salesmanship in the quest for winning pointers, provided we beware of those salesmanship manuals which teach salesmen to regard their prospects as mug 'punters'.

Winners never treat other people as 'mugs', but always as winners or potential winners – after all who wants to deal with a loser?

Like really good salesmen, winners know people's names – or have worked out useful ploys like 'Oh! I know your first name of course, it's your second names I've forgotten', or vice versa – because they realise that people's names are among their most prized attributes.

HOW TO REMEMBER NAMES

It is virtually impossible to remember the names of more than two people when you are introduced for the first time. Awkward introductions at a party are a classic case. It is extremely difficult and embarrassing when a host introduces you to a group.

You will have a winning chance if you know some of the names before you arrive. It is much easier to put faces to names than names to faces. Find out who is going to be at the gathering and write down and *memorise* the names before arriving.

Also find out the first names as well as the surnames. It is much easier to remember Nick Thornely rather than J. N. Thornely or Molly Lees rather than Mrs Lees. It is easier to remember first names as they sometimes give you a clue to character. Sue, Pandora, Mary, Johnny, Sam, Walter all give you some picture in your mind. This practice will help you remember the name. Remembering people's names will give you a great feeling of achievement and this is a winning characteristic.

When writing to people, there is never any excuse for spelling their name wrongly. To spell someone's name wrongly is a losing characteristic. If you have already received a letter from them then the signature is a vital clue as it has never been known for a person to spell their own name wrongly. The telephone directory is a good source too as printing errors are very rare.

Most Americans are much better than the British at remembering names, but tend to be obsessive about repeating them. A couple of repetitions should enable you to remember a name and it does help if you are discussing the person with a third party to refer to him as Fred Bloggs from Wrigglethorpe's and not as Whosit from Whatsit's.

Keeping business cards of people you meet can be a winning move, but try not to finish up with a pocket full of meaningless cards. This can happen easily at parties – oh yes, it can! – so try to scribble a couple of words on the back of the card to remind you of the person and the circumstances. However, if you write something like 'pompous

Americans are good with names

prat' on the back of someone's card, be careful to keep it safely hidden!

Incidentally, if you have an interesting or unusual name make the most of it. Find out if it is Norman French, Viking, Serbo Croatian or whatever because that can make your name memorable and a memorable name can help to make you a winner.

IT'S WHAT YOU KNOW ABOUT WHO YOU KNOW

Remembering names is only one way of 'stroking' and, of course, people feel even more like winners if you can remember what they do and a few other things about them, like their wife's name, what the kids are doing and so on.

It may seem calculating but since even some winners have terrible memories, an extended contacts book can be very useful. In fact, we should think in terms of preparing a winner's contacts book with notes on the people we meet – including people who work for us on a casual service basis – with not only the basic details, but also a listing of their likes and dislikes.

Most of us don't even have available all the information we need about our friends and relations and while business directories like Yellow Pages or Talking Pages can be immensely useful, the sort of thing a winner finds it worthwhile to know about, say, the mechanic who did such a great job on the family car is that he's a darts fanatic or dab hand at French cuisine.

Getting on well with people is a real help when it comes to being a winner and, once you have made a good start at the first encounter, it's a shame to waste it for the sake of making a couple of notes.

CONTACTS IN THE WORKPLACE

If contacts in the social context are important they are doubly so in the workplace where what people do is often considered to be more important than what they are.

Winners don't necessarily agree with this and their business contacts book should reflect this by containing not only 'name, rank and number' but a certain amount of personal information. Don't try to collect all the information at once, unless of course it is volunteered, and fill in the entries in your contacts book as soon after the meeting as possible.

PRACTICAL WINNERS

Lay out a contacts book with appropriate columns to include not only such items as name, address, occupation, title, phone number but also wife's name, children's names, birthdays, hobbies, affiliations, clubs, politics, not forgetting to leave space for comments like 'knowledgeable about computers' or 'wife runs cooking school'.

ROYAL WINNING

If you think making notes of this sort is 'sneaky' you may be interested to know that the Queen uses a very similar system – with a little help from her staff – and that people who are presented to her are often amazed and flattered to discover how much she knows about them, especially if she has met them on a previous occasion. This is stroking of a very high order and it works.

COMPLIMENTS

Remembering people's names and a few details about them, although absolutely essential, is a very elementary form of stroking compared to the delicate art of the compliment. People love compliments and are willing to believe almost anything good about themselves but as most winners realise instinctively, in the end insincere compliments can be counter-productive.

People love to be complimented on things like their dress, their appearance or their possessions and a winner should be able to use a genuine compliment to take the sting out of criticism. For example, a secretary who tells the office boy whose whistling is preventing her from getting on with her work 'My! Henry – you do sound cheerful this morning' is going to stand a better chance of persuading him to stop, than if she had said something like 'For God's sake, will you cut out that racket'.

Praise should be genuine and the winner's motto should be 'If you can't praise, at least don't knock'.

RECEIVING A COMPLIMENT

Many people are confused and embarrassed to be on the receiving end of a compliment. People blush, stammer and have even been known to contradict the *giver* of the compliment.

There is a simple response which is always pleasing and acceptable. If someone says 'You're looking good today' just smile and say 'Thank you'. Why argue? Enjoy the feeling of being a winner.

PRAISE IN THE WORKPLACE

In the workplace, as elsewhere, too much praise tends to debase the coinage but, if you have people working for you, you could find something on which to compliment them, even a small thing, once every day. Encouragement in the morning followed by praise in the afternoon is good winning strategy. It's much better to send people home smiling than scowling because the impression they take away from work, whether good or bad, is going to last – and perhaps grow. You could also find that in looking for something for which to praise people you discover that you really have got a winning team working for you which can only make you more of a winner.

Everyone loves a genuine compliment and winners use them to leave other people feeling like winners even if they have to criticise something. 'I like the way you've set that out – but . . .' is a typical winner's solution to the problem of telling people you think they are wrong. So *get the compliment habit but remember, it's like watering plants – essential, but it's a mistake to overdo it.*

STROKING THE BOSS

Complimenting people who hold higher positions in the workplace can be tricky because there's the obvious risk that you could be suspected, whether by the boss or your colleagues, of being a creep, which is definitely not the attribute of a winner. This is unfortunate because it puts many people off saying anything remotely pleasant to their boss which means that they could lose ideal opportunities to make the boss feel a winner.

Any compliments you pay to the boss should be absolutely genuine and, if anything, a shade less frequent than those paid to other people in your department.

Most bosses like to be complimented on their business expertise, their successes and even their acquisitions – which they like to feel they deserve – so your stroking will normally be welcome. However, if your boss seems too remote for that sort of compliment he would be unlikely to be upset by an oblique compliment like 'I wish I had your magic touch with clients' – always providing it's true.

PRACTICAL WINNING

Different strokes for different folks, as they say – but you might care to begin by verbally stroking your partner, if you have one, always remembering that to be effective compliments must be sincere. 'That was a delicious meal' or for that matter 'a really good bit of positive driving' could lead to a home win – often the most valuable of all.

As we have seen there are 'different strokes for different folks', but there are not many people who don't respond well to the knowledge that they and their efforts are appreciated. After practising stroking on your nearest and dearest – your partners, parents or siblings – move on to compliment colleagues and see how it helps turn you, and them, into winners. Note too how, if you have not been given to appreciative comments in the past, a few words of praise will usually cause the person concerned to try even harder. Of course, your praise should be sincere, so practice looking for things to praise and you could soon find yourself a winner – in a family of winners.

Tip from the Top

'You never get a second chance to make a good first impression.'

5

WINNERS CAN'T BE LOSERS

Winning is a cumulative affair – so much so that it is often difficult to decide which came first, the winning chicken or the prize egg – and this is one reason why it is so important to get the winning habit, to start winning in small things, to achieve minor goals and reach intermediate targets. Once you get the winning ball rolling, it is like a snowball on a hill covered in soft snow, small at first but gradually becoming larger as it picks up more snow until it becomes huge and unstoppable.

At the same time winners begin to behave like winners in their dealings with other people and, once again, it's a little difficult to tell after a while whether they are behaving in a courteous and considerate fashion *because* they are winners or whether it is the way they behave to other people that makes them winners.

The answer, we believe, is that the real winner – the sort of winner we are talking about in this book – is a holistic winner, a complete winning personality to whom winning comes as naturally as breathing. He doesn't have to think about whether he is going to be polite or considerate to people in the workplace, for instance, because knowing he is a winner gives him unshakeable confidence *even when things go wrong.*

THE CONFIDENCE TRICK

Once you have played the game of spot the winner a couple of times – especially in the workplace – it's easy to see that winners are confident and unafraid while losers tend to be fearful. Not that winners go around talking tough to the boss for example: quite the opposite in fact. They are as polite to the boss as they are to everyone else. It's merely that they know they could be tough if the occasion arose – and so does everyone else.

The remarkable thing is how little time it takes, once you have decided to become a winner, to acquire this special sort of confidence which, of course, marks you out as a winner and helps you win even more.

The secret lies in what the military experts call the **worst possible scenario**. As we shall see, motivation specialists use a different term for the Worst Possible Scenario and for what they see as the Best Possible Scenario, but for the moment let's stick with the WPS which, as its name implies, refers to the very worst that could happen in any given situation and incorporates Sod's Law which states 'Anything which can go wrong will go wrong'.

Obviously, the winner's confidence derives in part from the fact that he is good at his job, which he enjoys because it is just at the right level to stretch him without causing him stress and because he is well liked by his colleagues and his bosses. However, this doesn't completely explain the impression he gives of being completely impervious to the slings and arrows of commercial politics and industrial misfortune.

In fact his confidence is largely due to the fact that he has already examined the worst possible scenarios and faced up to the worst that could happen to him in his present situation. He has also made contingency plans, however tenuous, to deal with such situations should they ever arise.

PRACTICAL WINNING: WORST POSSIBLE SCENARIO

Try working out your own Worst Possible Scenario. Make a list of total disasters you might conceivably have to face, beginning with dreadful happenings in the workplace. Don't worry about grading them at the moment – you can place them in order of sheer horror later on. Of course, everyone's list will be different, but there will be a few common factors like losing one's source of income.

One person's list might look something like this:

YOUR FIRM GOES BANKRUPT
YOU ARE FIRED
YOUR BOSS LEAVES AND YOU CANNOT WORK FOR THE NEW ONE
YOUR FIRM IS TAKEN OVER AND ONE OF THE JOBS TO GO IS YOURS

These are all serious and often very real sources of anxiety, but if you examine them it's obvious that they are all fundamentally the *same worry*, namely that you are going to lose your job. Now winners, by definition, are less likely to lose their jobs than non-winners but, of course, they could do so. They don't think *it could never happen to me.* However, winners – while certainly not worriers – do practise *worst scenario management* which means that instead of concerning themselves with *four* unpleasant possibilities, some of which they can do very little about, they concern themselves with only *one* major disaster, i.e. the possibility that they may lose their job.

WORRY MANAGEMENT

For the sake of convenience we may refer to this as Worry Management and, as it can save a lot of sleepless nights – not to mention ulcers – it is a definite step towards becoming a winner.

With only one disaster to think about, the winner can set about making plans to cope with it, which in this case – once you have taken all possible steps not to lose your job – means making sure that you have a parachute.

WINNERS HAVE PARACHUTES

Winners, of course, are less likely to be fired than losers anyway because they will have made many friends in their own organisation and outside it. Their friends inside their own organisation may not be able to help them keep the job they hold at the moment but they could, particularly if the organisation is a large one, suggest and perhaps implement a sideways or even temporarily downwards move.

PARACHUTE ONE

Prepare a C.V. and keep it up to date. It's wonderful how much more of a winner you will sound when you know it's only in fun, but it will be there if ever you need it. In the same way, keep a list of firms in your own line of work and write a couple of draft letters of application. Once again, when it's in fun you'll find you come over as the winner you are. However, don't leave the draft letters lying around!

If the worst happens you'll be very fortunate, even as a winner, to walk into a new job straight away, especially the exact job you want. Winners, of course, do tend to walk into *better* jobs than the ones they have lost but, while you can hope for this to happen, you can't count on it and it makes sense to think of short term solutions.

PARACHUTE TWO

If you were to be offered a different job in your present firm, decide which jobs you could do and would enjoy and, consequently, which you would be prepared to accept – perhaps even on a temporary basis.

Winners tend to have good contacts in other organisations similar to their own which they built up by friendliness, fair dealing and, let's face it, by keeping up with the gossip which, being winners, they are well placed to do.

PARACHUTE THREE

Make a list of contacts in firms similar to your own, together with office and home phone numbers where appropriate. A little gentle sounding out might not come amiss and winners can strike just the right note of ever-so-slightly-serious banter with this one.

Winners have their ears to the ground and are less likely to be caught out on any given 'Night of the Long Envelopes' but these things can happen quickly and it's as well to be prepared.

PARACHUTE FOUR

Think of a temporary job you could do while looking around. A commission-only selling job is a good bet in this respect as it brings in money quickly which prevents reserves becoming exhausted and, as salesmen usually make their own hours, leaves you free to tackle the job situation in your own field without pressure. We are talking about direct selling here: if you can knock on somebody's door and sell them something, you need never worry about losing your job again and that alone puts you well on the way to being a winner.

Most winners can sell – most really good salesmen are winners anyway – so selling is an extremely useful parachute, so much so that it is a skill worth acquiring. If you have a daytime job which leaves you with your evenings and perhaps weekends free, take a part-time selling job for a month or so. Nowadays there is very little cold canvassing. Salesmen are given 'qualified' leads to prospects who have expressed interest in the product or service on offer and most firms will provide some training.

Proving that you can sell not only provides a parachute – as well as paying for a new car or a holiday – but also makes you more of a winner in the workplace in as much as it is a great boost to one's confidence, enabling the winner to extend a purely imaginery two-fingered salute in the direction of the firm's resident Himmler.

Selling of course is not the only alternative income parachute.

PARACHUTE FIVE

Make a list of jobs you could do at a pinch, ranging from fairly down-to-earth occupations like tele-sales, temping or working in a shop to driving a lorry or becoming a dustman. Don't worry if some of the jobs you think of seem a bit lowly or off-beat. If the jobs are available and you can do them it does mean that you and your family are unlikely to starve. Starving is, after all, what you are really worrying about when you worry about losing your job – starving and being without a roof over your head – but in fact the worst that could happen is that your lifestyle might be altered dramatically. In fact, living on very little money is not too difficult and can be something of a challenge *provided* that you have enough for basics and, most importantly, *provided* that the situation is *temporary* and that you *know* things are going to get better.

PARACHUTE SIX

Make a plan for living on the absolute minimum possible amount of money, distinguishing carefully between what you *want* and what you really *need*. Think in terms of selling assets – remember this is all hypothetical. You could, for instance, manage with a smaller house but would perhaps need to keep your car – if it belongs to you – for use in a new job or for transport to help you find a new position. In this connection it might be worthwhile, if you can afford it, to buy a reasonable 'old banger' as a second car, to reduce the trauma should you lose the firm's car.

Plan for an alternative lifestyle in case the worst should happen

List any other 'parachutes' that may occur to you. For example, if your partner is not currently employed you could discuss with them the possibility of their taking a job for a while, should you lose your position. Partners should usually be involved in the Worst Possible Scenario planning from the start and obviously well before there is any chance of the WPS being realised. When it is all a game rather than a reality, both of you may come up with ideas for unusual 'parachutes' like turning what is now a hobby into a paying proposition.

Having dealt with a major worry, winners can use the Worst Possible Scenario technique to deal with most of life's disquieting features both in the workplace and at home. It is surprising how many worries vanish completely, for example, when you apply the principles of Worry Management, one of which is not to worry about things you cannot possibly do anything about, such as the earth being destroyed by a runaway comet. If you think that's silly, by the way, try making a list of your illogical worries of the week – and then stop worrying about them.

Winners do not worry too much because they have made contingency plans. Winners can afford to be independent, confident and fearless and therefore are less likely to lose their jobs in the first place. It's the chicken and the egg question again, but who cares which comes first – being a winner or winning – when all that really matters is that *winners rarely lose.*

Tip from the Top

'Every problem is an opportunity.'

6

PLANNING TO WIN

If you aim to win it's as well to have a plan. It's no use thinking in a vague sort of way of winning 'one of these days'. This is one of the besetting sins of many people who look as if they ought to be winners, but who are still 'coming men' when they collect their gold watch.

The fact is that, no matter what sort of person you are, it does pay to have a plan but remember, *a plan is a plan* – just that and no more. It is not an immutable timetable, deviation from which will render the planner liable to be struck by thunderbolts. A rigid schedule which makes no allowance for changing circumstances or the vagaries of other people is as constricting as a strait-jacket and is something with which no winner would wish to be associated.

Winners make lots of plans before deciding on one they think should be feasible and, partly because they have considered lots of plans before deciding on a course of action, they are ready – and able – to change plans if need be.

WINNERS DO DAY-DREAM

More heresy, but winners do day-dream and so they should. What winners do not do is day-dream all the time.

Remember a plan is only a plan

Day-dreaming is constructive – it allows a part of your brain to come into play which is not used at other times and which may come up with some brilliant ideas. However, the old-fashioned schoolteachers who regarded day-dreaming as a cardinal sin had some right on their side as day-dreaming can be addictive, mainly because it is so pleasant.

One way to get the best out of day-dreaming and at the same time avoid being hooked on it immoderately is to set aside times and places for the exercise and to refrain if possible from day-dreaming at other times. Some people find the bath an ideal place for day-dreaming and certainly the tub has a useful reputation when it comes to generating ideas. Other people find that the few minutes before they drift off to sleep is a good time, but this does have disadvantages as it is quite possible to wake up next morning remembering only that you had a marvellous idea, but without the slightest recollection of what it was. In fact, it's not a bad idea, even in the bath, to day-dream with a notebook and pencil to hand. In bed, people with partners are doubly fortunate – a quick nudge from an elbow turns them into instant tape recorders. But you can't get too mad at them if they forget your brilliant idea.

DIRECT YOUR DREAMS

The Germans call day-dreams '*wunschtraüme*' or 'wish dreams' and this is exactly what winners' day-dreams should be because it implies that you can guide them in a specific direction.

This is not to say undirected day-dreams can't be fun, or even productive, but winners should direct at least some of their day-dreams. This is, of course, quite fun too as it involves imagining how great it would be if you had already won.

DAY-DREAMS ARE THE RAW MATERIAL OF PLANS

Day-dreams, and especially those of the *wunschtraüme* variety, are really the first steps in planning. They are a game of 'How nice it would be if . . .' and in the first instance the only restriction to your dreams is the scope of your imagination, though for most people there is an undercurrent of logic in their day-dreaming which is not always present in dreaming proper, so that day-dreams hover on the fringe of the possible.

'If wishes were horses beggars would ride' was the way our friend, the old-fashioned schoolmaster, put it. But in fact a beggar wishing for a horse is a lot closer to riding than a beggar to whom the idea has not occurred. Wishing for a horse or, for that matter, a car, a house, an aeroplane or a new and better job, and dreaming how pleasant it would be to have our wishes come true is the first step in planning to *make* them come true.

The next step occurs while still in the day-dreaming mode, as it were, as vague plans begin to emerge, some of which may well be absolute nonsense. Kidnapping the Chairman at gun point for example is not perhaps the best way to go about getting a raise or even a parking spot in the firm's car park. However, as you continue to day-dream, you may stumble on a plan which is much less ludicrous and perhaps even several such plans.

MAKING DREAMS COME TRUE

Day-dreaming, even constructive day-dreaming, is not enough by itself and we now need to take a good look at some of the plans we have come up with while our minds were relaxed. It's not a bad idea to examine even the most bizarre, way-out ideas in the cold light of the office in case there is the germ of a real plan lurking amongst the wild schemes. Then pick the plan you like best and work through it on paper taking care to map out several intermediate stages.

Now take this plan – call it Plan A if you want to be original – back to the day-dreaming stage to see if your subconscious will come up with any further inspiration. At no stage should you totally reject Plans B, C, D etc. because they could come in handy later on. *Winners do change horses in mid-stream* if the horse they are riding weakens.

Most winners do this sort of pre-planning without even being aware of it. If you have never used the day-dreaming part of your mind, you are missing out on a valuable weapon in the winner's armoury but don't worry, it is an easy skill to acquire.

Winners let their minds wander – after all they could come back with a treasure trove.

Apart from going back to our day-dreams from time to time for a fantasy top-up and to pick up possible new ideas, it is now time for us to bring our conscious minds into play and one of the best ways of moving from the day-dreaming mode to the conscious mode is to write things down. This is not to say that we shouldn't make notes of any bright ideas we derive from our day-dreams; of course we should, and the sooner the better, but in the planning mode writing things down becomes much more purposeful.

WHAT DO YOU WANT TO ACHIEVE?

You have now had time to sort out your dreams and to decide what it is that you really want and what *you* feel will make you a winner. You have also had the opportunity to engage in *wish management* – much the same way as we tackled Worry Management – by grouping our wishes together where appropriate and by deciding on which major wish is achievable. For instance, if we wish for a new house, a new car or a diamond necklace what we are really wishing for is more money; if we wish to be admired, respected, loved, to have more friends at work and out of it, what we are really wishing for is more personal success.

WINNERS WISH FOR THE MOON

'Don't wish for the moon' was the advice the old-fashioned schoolmaster handed out, sometimes because he genuinely didn't wish his pupils to be disappointed, but more often because he had always kept his own feet firmly on the ground and was jealous of anyone he thought might reach for the moon. For him, wanting to be an executive was fine but wanting to found a new company was over-ambitious. The people who became winners were those who took no notice of this particular advice.

PRACTICAL WINNING

Winners set their sights at the limits of what they consider to be achievable. To impress on themselves – and perhaps their partner if they have one – the fact that they really do think they can achieve the goals they are setting, they plan to achieve them in readily grasped segments of time. That is to say, if you aim to lose weight as part of a major *goal group* of making yourself more attractive then aim to lose three pounds in a month rather than three stone in a year and so on. If your goal is to re-organise your office as part of a major *goal group* of making yourself more efficient in the workplace plan to do so in two months *not* 'some time soon'.

Write down your plan but once again, remember it is only a plan and not a set of laws, whether it is a purely personal plan or somehow involves other people, especially subordinates. Winners are not obsessive – they know that plans are guidelines.

With this in mind, plans should include intermediate goals and each achievement of a minor goal should be celebrated as a *win*! This is important and we'll be reminding ourselves of it from time to time, partly because intermediate goals direct us towards the particular slice of moon we are wishing for in a positive manner. But most important of all, if for some reason, and it could be ill-health or an accident, we don't get the moon we are wishing for we won't be too disappointed because we will have had all those splendid wins along the way, and we'll know we have done all that was possible to make our dreams come true.

WINNERS WRITE THINGS DOWN

Writing – the ability to make a permanent record – was perhaps the most important factor in the advance of civilisation and today the emphasis is on data collection and information technology.

We all know that 'knowledge is power' but do we write down everything we need to remember or put it into our computer? Do we hell! We rely on the power of our infallible memories to remember everything from whether we put the cat out and switched the gas off, to the telephone number of the one person who could make us rich and famous. Don't worry – even most winners tend to place too much reliance on their memories. But winners still have more helpful information at their fingertips than non-winners.

PRACTICAL WINNING

The winner's bible – the contacts book. We've talked about lists of contacts but now is the time to start a contacts book – not merely an address book but a real contacts book – with all the pertinent information about the people we meet, and maybe even a bit of gossip. If you don't already have a suitable book, buy a good one that's meant to last and with lots of space. Make sure you write down the name and address of every new contact you make plus a short identifying note and cross references where appropriate, for example:

Bloggs Fred (address, phone number) sales rep for Papertrade PLC – keen gardener – wife social worker – good man to deal with.

When people give you their business cards make a note on the back of each one as soon as you can saying where you met and any relevant information not on the card, for example, 'John's party – int. in buying car' or 'Club – could be client'. Do *not* write 'Met in Bull's Head – wimp'. By all means note people's less pleasing characteristics where relevant but, when you do so, use a simple – and deniable – personal code.

As we mentioned, making this sort of note, especially on the cards you pick up on social occasions, will save you from finishing up with a pocket full of cards with no idea where you met the people concerned or what you talked about. Transfer the information to your contacts book as soon as possible and have a small pocket address/contacts book in which to jot down information on people who don't give you cards.

DEAR DIARY

Keep a full and accurate diary and write it up *daily* as well as using it for appointments. Winners not only know where they are going – they know where they have been and what happened because only in this way can they chart their wins and analyse the odd occasion on which they didn't win in order not to make the same mistake again.

PRACTICAL WINNING: LIST MAKING – A WINNING HABIT

Loads of lists means loads of wins – but for the moment think in terms of listing your jobs and goals for the day and tick off each one as it is completed. Enjoy the sense of accomplishment: *you are winning* with each job you tick off.

While the idea of being a winner is a relatively new one keep a list *at home* of the times you have proved to be a winner during the day and also the times you might have been more of a winner – and why. Don't brood – just make a note of how you could have done better. Very soon you'll find that winning is the rule and the rare times on which you don't win will be real surprises – in fact you'll even find yourself laughing about them.

At work keep lists recording wins by your team and department, both collective and individual. They can be a real morale booster especially at times when extra effort is indicated.

LIVE BY THE LISTS NOT FOR THE LISTS

Don't become obsessive! Lists, like plans, are there to help you become a winner so don't make more lists or plans than you can comfortably handle. Lists and plans are designed to save winners work because *work is something winners hate* and are determined to give up as far as is possible.

Tip from the Top

'No one plans to fail, but many fail to plan.'
'A plan is a dream with a deadline.'

7

WINNERS DON'T WHINE

What winners say is important, but often it's how they say it that makes all the difference. The way you speak can be one of the most important factors in making you a winner. Listen to someone you have already identified as a winner and ten to one he or she will be speaking clearly, distinctly and with interesting variations in pitch and tone.

Above all they will be speaking with quiet confidence. 'Quiet', because real winners do not have to bellow all the time although some of them have been known to shout when appropriate. Usually they find it quite sufficient to project their voices as actors do and you will usually find that in a social gathering, for example, although the winner may not be talking more loudly than the other people – often in fact quite the opposite – it will be the winner's voice that you hear clearly among all the conversational 'rhubarb'.

WINNING ACCENTS – ARE YOU STRANGLED BY THE OLD SCHOOL TIE?

Some years ago there was an advertisement that appeared in a great many papers and magazines – for all we know it may still appear – which ran 'Are you strangled by the Old School Tie when the power to speak could free you?'

The implication was that if you had not been to a public school you were disadvantaged and learning how to speak correctly could redress the balance. In those days 'correctly' meant with a standard English or public school accent and a couple of decades or so ago it was absolutely true that anyone who didn't speak standard English was handicapped while anyone who spoke the public school version of standard English was privileged.

Of course, no-one can say that, in England at any rate, this form of snobbery no longer exists. It does, and in certain circumstances it is no bad thing to be able to speak standard English. However, thanks largely to radio and TV, regional accents have become acceptable and some, in fact, very acceptable indeed. Scottish has always been more acceptable than most other accents but now Welsh and Irish are perfectly okay in Britain and in some places in the world a great deal more acceptable than an English accent.

Nowadays a regional accent is no bar to becoming a winner. Besides, it is easy enough to become bilingual if you wish and winners are often linguistic chameleons who adapt their accent to the company and the circumstances. Everyone does this to some extent by modifying their accent and the way they speak – not to mention what they say – when they are out with friends as compared with, say, at home or in the workplace.

Winners merely develop this ability which is often a question of shading, rather than changing one's accent completely. You don't have to speak perfect Scouse, for example, to be accepted in a Liverpool pub, but if you have a Public School accent you might find it politic to modify it slightly. In other words being 'Strangled by the Old School

Tie' now has a whole new meaning and it is the wearers rather than the non-wearers who find they have to modify their speech if they move out of the Old School environment.

This they will almost certainly have to do if they wish to become real winners because *winners are socially mobile.*

ACCENTUATE THE ACCENT

The main thing winners have to learn is not to be worried or ashamed about whatever accent they may have. If you are worried about the way you speak, change it. If you find you are unable to change it make a feature of it so that it becomes a part of your personality, as a number of top TV personalities, not to mention film stars, do these days. You could decide to retain your accent as your trademark but – and this is a big 'but' – if you decide to retain your accent this is no excuse for speaking badly. After all, the purpose of speaking is to get your meaning across and a voice which sounds as if you are speaking through your nose whilst eating a giant hamburger will not do it.

Winners' voices are never monotonous, whatever their accent: in fact a monotonous whine – think of the whinging Pom – rather unfairly tags you as a loser. So if you have a real whine in your voice, lose it! It not only makes you a loser but makes everyone you speak to feel like a loser too. Don't worry – as you begin to be more of a winner the whine will vanish automatically, but try to speed things up if you possibly can. Incidentally, if you have a speech impediment this is no longer the drawback it once was and you can take comfort from the large number of radio and TV personalities who began life with similar handicaps.

SHOCK! HORROR! CAN THAT BE ME?

You may not even know what your voice sounds like, in which case you are certainly in for a surprise, if not a shock, because people's voices invariably sound different to other people from the way they hear them themselves and therefore from the way they imagine they sound.

Ask someone with a tape recorder to record some of your ordinary conversation, if possible when you are not aware they are doing so, and then play it back. Your first reaction could well be that of many broadcasters on hearing themselves for the first time, namely 'That can't be me'. It is!

Now you know what you sound like and, if you are unhappy with what you hear, you can use the tape recorder to help you modify the way you speak. You will almost certainly, for instance, wish to speak more clearly because *winners can't win unless they get their winning message across.*

A SELLING PITCH

Male winners may wish to pitch their voices a little deeper than they are when they first hear themselves on tape. This is only a question of practice. In the same way, many women may find they wish to speak a little more softly. Using the voice correctly is an essential weapon in the winner's armoury in most circumstances, but it is also an acceptable way of using sex in social and working situations.

Think of a few ways in which you have used your voice recently to help you get what you want – in other words to be a winner – or times when having a more attractive voice might have been useful. Winners find that attractive speaking voices help make them winners all through the day for every day of their lives and they don't even have to think about it. So, if your voice needs changing, use the tape recorder to help you change it.

LEARNING TO READ

Oh really! This is too much. I wouldn't have bought the book if I hadn't been able to read.

Quite right – you can read; most of us can, but can you get words off a page? Try reading a few paragraphs from a newspaper, a poem or a play script, which you can borrow from your local library, into a tape recorder – you can practise first if you like. Then play it back and you will realise why even some professional actors occasionally find it difficult to 'get words off the page'.

Reading aloud is an art and a particularly useful one for winners so even if it sounds stiff and unnatural at first, do persevere. If you find it embarrassing even though you are by yourself try using 'funny' voices to make yourself laugh before going on. Later you may wish to use your partner, if you have one, as a sounding board to check your progress and to comment. Whatever you do, keep the first tapes you make. They could give you a giggle – and a genuine sense of achievement – when you play them back in a week or so's time.

Don't forget, if you already have a 'good' accent and perfect speaking voice as well as superb delivery you may wish to use the recorder to help with your ability to modify these factors when appropriate.

WINNING ROLES

Try playing out imaginary scenes featuring your colleagues and bosses in different situations. Imagine, for instance, that you are in the boss's office discussing your request for something fairly minor – say a car space or a new drinks machine for the office. Try it once with the boss in a good mood and once with the boss in a foul temper.

Remember you are concentrating on getting your voice right but, at the same time, bear in mind that winners are expert at what may be called *verbal judo*. The art of judo involves using the strength of the other person's attack against him and verbal judo works in much the same way. Winners do *not* say 'You are absolutely wrong' – they *do* say 'You could be right but I've given it a lot of thought and . . .' or 'What you say is very interesting but . . .'. Try to convey this attitude by your tone of voice rather than words, using the tape recorder to check the impression you hope to make.

WAITER, THERE'S SOME SOUP ON MY FLY

Again, using the recorder, intersperse the workplace scenes with other imaginary situations. For example: you are complaining about the food or the service in a restaurant. Winners are less likely than losers to get either bad service or bad food, but it can happen. Winners, however, are completely at ease in such situations because they realise that restaurant staff are – if only on a temporary basis – their employees and, since they know how to get the best out of the people who work with and for them, there should be no problem.

Accepting partial responsibility is not a bad move. 'Oh waiter. I appear to have mislaid my soup spoon' is the sort of thing that can be useful when the dereliction is not serious, while 'I'm sorry, I should have made it clear I wanted my steak really well cooked' deals with a slightly more serious error. Remember, the aim of the exercise as always is to get what you want – not to make the other chap, in this case the waiter, feel small or aggrieved or to panic him into making further mistakes. Keep your voice calm but firm and smile as you talk – even into the tape recorder.

Try this sort of scene once or twice and then play out a scene in which the waiter is stroppy – say about the bill – and you have to send for the manager: 'I think I'd better have a word with the manager' being more of a winner's phrase than 'Get me the bloody manager'. When the imaginary manager arrives 'I wonder if you could help us straighten this out' could be a useful start.

You could also try, for example, placating a large lorry driver after your parked car has kept him blocked in a side street for half an hour: 'How stupid of me! Whatever could I have been thinking of?'.

Use the tape recorder whenever you can and try injecting into the same line a note of firmness, humour, confidence and so on until you feel you have it just right for the occasion.

MAN'S BEST FRIEND – THE DOG AND BONE

When it comes to winning, one of Man's best friends – and Woman's too – is the telephone and it can help you be a winner both in the workplace and in the social sphere.

Winners tend to use the phone a great deal, not only because it is quick and convenient, but because it is a first class way of bringing their winning personalities to bear. Also, while they don't use the phone to deceive people in any unpleasant way, winners are fully aware of the fact that the phone enables them to present themselves in the best possible light at times when a personal confrontation might be less flattering.

Winners, for example, seldom get hangovers, but you could imagine an occasion on which you feel really rough because of a cold or a hangover and practice projecting on the phone the impression of a fit, confident individual, bright-eyed, bushy-tailed – and definitely a winner.

Most of the time, however, the winner will use the phone in a more straightforward way to achieve whatever it is he wishes. To do this, he makes use of a curious fact of electronics which you have probably noticed in your experiments with the tape recorder, namely that electronic equipment accentuates vocal characteristics, accents and above all emotions. This is particularly true of the telephone which can pick up fear or indecision quicker than a lie detector and at the same time is capable of accentuating a speaker's feeling of happiness or confidence. In fact, a telephone can even pick up a smile, which is why winners spend a lot of time smiling into the phone. So much so that a winner using the phone when he's in good form could easily be mistaken for something of a headcase.

This is because the winner is acting into the phone – smiling, shaking his head, frowning and so on as though the person at the other end of the line were sitting at the other side of the desk.

This is the winning way to use the phone and once you have mastered it you will never look back.

Project your personality on the phone

PRACTICAL WINNING

Using the tape recorder and an unplugged phone try using the acting-into-the-phone technique to persuade a colleague to change his day off, to ask your boss a favour you know he won't be too happy to grant or to tell your best beloved you won't be able to get home for your anniversary.

DON'T FORGET TO PHONE

As we have stressed, winners use the phone a lot and this is partly because phones build up brownie points at work and on the home front. This doesn't mean that you have to be on the phone either to your boss or your loved one every five minutes, but people do like to be kept informed. You can be the best salesman in the world for instance, but if you are in the field and lose contact with the office for days at a time you are going to give your boss ulcers, which is not a winning move. At the same time, your wife or husband is going to forgive almost anything provided he or she knows that you have not run off with a new lover – or been flattened by a bus.

AND FINALLY – THE FIRST WORD

A lot of people who on all other occasions use the phone like winners by really projecting their personalities answer the phone with a colourless 'Hello' as though they were about to expire at any moment. Winners know that a

'Hello' sets the tone of the whole conversation that follows and could in fact be an all-important first contact with – who knows – a talent scout who's looking for a genuine winner. Answer the phone with a cheerful 'Hello!' or even 'Good Morning, Fred Bloggs . . .' and use the recorder to test the impression you make – it should be one that will help to make you a winner.

Tip from the Top

'Communicate to accumulate.'

8

FIT TO WIN

Being a winner means being in control of ourselves, of events and of other people. As we have seen, we can begin to get the winning habit by taking control of our own lives in such seemingly trivial areas as deciding the time at which we get up in the morning.

What we have done by getting up earlier is to begin winning by making decisions in an area in which we might be expected to have maximum control. We can now look for similar areas, one of which is our own body. Unless we are extremely ill, our body is one thing about which we and we alone take decisions so it is an area in which we *can* win; so much so that even some prisoners, who have lost control over virtually every other aspect of their lives, take an interest in building up their physique as being one of the areas in which they can still win.

YOU TOO CAN HAVE A BODY

You don't have to be a top class athlete to be a winner, but athletes do tend to be winners in other spheres than their own sport, largely because they are fit, poised and confident. In other words, they look and behave like winners. Fortunately most of us can attain fitness, poise and confidence without winning Olympic medals and, once we are reasonably fit, a few minutes a day is usually all the time it takes to maintain that air of physical well-being and mental alertness that says 'winner'.

THE BAD NEWS – AND THE GOOD NEWS

The bad news is that you may not be as 'reasonably' fit as you think you are because, unless you fall ill, being unfit creeps up on you without your realising it. The good news is that you can usually become much fitter without giving up all the good things in life.

One way of finding out exactly how fit you are is to have a full scale medical check-up, but that can be fairly expensive. Alternatively, you could ask your own doctor to run the rule over you to make sure that there is nothing radically and obviously wrong and then do a test at a reputable fitness centre.

Naturally, these people are after your business but they will give you a test, usually for a small set fee, and let you know how fit you are and how you could improve. You could even find that it is worthwhile joining a fitness centre, but try to get a week or so on a trial basis before committing yourself to a full year.

GO FOR THE GLOW

When it comes to physical exercise, winners don't 'go for the burn' – instead they go for the 'glow' that comes from exercising without strain and well within one's capabilities. The secret is that, like all winning, it has to be fun and the fun lies in feeling one's capabilities extend from day to day.

As we know from personal experience, it is possible even for people who have let themselves go completely to regain a good level of fitness in a matter of a couple of months. In fact, the programme detailed in *The Champagne Fitness Book* by Dan Lees (Redcliffe Press) can achieve tremendous results in only 90 days but if, like the author was when he started, you are several stone overweight and really unfit, this does need a certain amount of time and dedication.

Anyone who has not let themselves go completely and can spare, say, half an hour to an hour each day could anticipate excellent results in the course of six months. After that, about two hours in total each week should be enough to maintain fitness, although to tell the truth, once you have reached a peak of bubbly Champagne Fitness, you may not wish to restrict the time you spend on exercise or sport. In fact it is the cumulative effect once again.

When it is a question of taking control of your body, *the more you win, the more you want to go on winning.*

CHAMPAGNE FITNESS

Aim to achieve the ebullient champagne sparkle that goes with glowing health by combining a diet of tasty and interesting food and drink with a course of exercise which is sufficiently varied not to be boring. Boredom is the enemy of the winner and boredom is the curse of many diets and exercise programmes. The great thing about aiming for the sort of fitness we describe is that you can actually feel – and see – yourself winning.

Achieving the sort of fitness we are talking about does involve dieting if you are overweight but, in much the same way as we advise winners to work less rather than more, we advise people who want to lose weight to eat and drink better things rather than starve themselves.

A WINNING DIET

Living on lettuce leaves and water is a concept totally abhorrent to winners so we advise eating and drinking the best of everything.

This brings into play two limiting factors insofar as (a) good food and drink cost more than stodge and (b) you don't need, and in fact usually do not want, to eat as much of the most nutritious food as you do stodge. As far as expense is concerned, the two factors cancel each other out as *small* quantities of excellent food and drink cost much the same as *large* quantities of less exciting food.

Of course, you will have reduced the amount you eat and drink but you will find it difficult to feel deprived or bored, which are the drawbacks of every other diet we have come across. A typical Champagne Fitness day, for example, will include a glass of champagne, fish cooked in white wine and usually a glass of wine with both lunch and dinner.

WINNING WORKOUTS

A winning workout should be something you enjoy so if, for instance, you like swimming, make a regular visit to the baths a major part of your workout programme. If, on the other hand, you hate swimming, but still appreciate that it is superb all round exercise, restrict it to a minor role in your workout programme.

Some exercise is boring beyond belief but, using the Judo technique which we have already mentioned as part of the winner's armoury, it is possible to turn even this to advantage. For example, if you are using an exercise bike – which is about as much fun as watching paint dry – you can use a cassette player to learn a foreign language. We know someone who picked up a University degree largely as a result of listening to tapes and reading while using an exercise bike and a rowing machine. Of course, it doesn't have to be a foreign language: you could use your exercise time to become an expert on the music of J. S. Bach or for that matter 'Jelly Roll' Morton.

This is a winning move in two ways because you are becoming an expert at something and therefore a winner, while the fact that you are not thinking about your exercising means that you will exercise more naturally and almost certainly for a longer time. In fact, we may instance

A real winner would pat the dog as well

this as yet another favourite axiom of the old-fashioned schoolmaster which doesn't stand up to close examination, namely their warning that it is wrong to try to do two things at once.

WINNERS INVARIABLY DO TWO OR MORE THINGS AT ONCE

Winners can't help doing more than one thing at once, mainly because almost every winning move they make has a knock-on effect, so that, for example, becoming fitter doesn't affect only our health – although this in itself is of vital importance. At the same time as we become fitter we gain in confidence, we change the way in which people look at us and, as our clothes hang better, we begin to look better dressed. We should also find that mentally we are a great deal more alert than when we were unfit. This is yet another example of the *snowball factor*.

It's obvious that even the lowliest member of an organisation can become a winner in this way by becoming a person glowing with health and vitality. Mind you, glowing is usually quite sufficient and it is not a winning move to do triple somersaults into your boss's office if he happens to be a sixty-five-year-old, twenty-stone, arthritis sufferer.

Winners do not show off. Of course, this doesn't mean that they pass up on opportunities to demonstrate their excellence or expertise, merely that they pick their moments. The firm's athletic teams, for example, can provide an ideal and acceptable winning showcase.

THE SNOWBALL EFFECT – AGAIN

Fitness is a typical example of the cumulative effect of winning and acquiring winning habits which we have variously referred to as the 'snowball effect' or the 'knock-on effect', in order to stress the fact that wins, however small, rarely occur in a vacuum, and that a win in one sphere will almost certainly lead to wins in others.

We can see this very clearly in the case of the spin-off wins we get as a bonus once we achieve 'Champagne Fitness'. We've noticed that we feel more alert and have a better posture and walk, all of which give us an immediate bonus in the workplace because it is something that other people, especially bosses, tend to notice. Another bonus is that our clothes feel better and look better – as well as, curiously enough, more expensive. Because of this, people tend to look on us more as winners than they may have done before, which encourages us to pursue a winning path.

Watch out for these bonus effects as you go through the book. We shall point out some of them, but you should be able to find others for yourself.

WINNERS EXCEL – AT SOME THINGS

Winners like to win things although they are not obsessively competitive. In other words, they like to win relatively easily and certainly without killing themselves in the process. 'Effortless' is the word that comes to mind when one thinks of sportsmen, for example, who are genuine winners.

Think up a few examples of your own. The people concerned may have spent a lot of time practising or training but they invariably look as though they are giving their best without giving up the ghost.

When you are reasonably fit you may wish to think in terms of taking up a sport. As emerges fairly clearly from *Beginner's Luck* by Dan Lees (Redcliffe Press) it is easy to take up practically any sort of sporting activity these days at whatever age, even if it is something you have never tried before. The facilities are usually close at hand and the people who have been interested in the particular sport for some time are invariably pleased to welcome a newcomer and to give all the support they can. In most cases club members, we found, were willing to lend equipment to enable beginners to try out the sport in question without going to any expense.

Of course, being a winner at abseiling or canoeing won't guarantee promotion in the workplace but these things *do* make you feel like a winner and they can also help develop latent powers of leadership – so much so that many large firms are now paying for their executives to take part in sports and more particularly in the Outward Bound type of activity which has a more immediate and obvious application in promoting leadership qualities useful in the workplace.

Being fit is fine, but don't worry if you are not the athletic type. A win is a win is a win and if you can become a champion at tiddleywinks or mumbledy peg you will still experience the 'rush' that comes from winning and go on to win more.

A WIN, IS A WIN, IS A WIN

The important thing in being a winner is to win and, outside the office or the workshop, there is a whole world in which to win and multifarious ways in which to become a winner. Imagine, for instance, that you were to take up an exotic and gentle form of unarmed combat and become a Brown or even a Black Belt. Come to think of it, even a Yellow Belt – which means you are considered just about teachable – is enough to make you walk tall.

Make a list of sports, hobbies and other activities you might wish to pursue, especially those about which you have always said 'I'd like to try my hand at that'.

____

____

____

A WIN IS A WIN – IS A PARACHUTE

You might even think about winning at a hobby, for example, which could make you a little money – so that, almost without thinking, you will not only have chalked up a win but at the same time prepared yourself the beginnings of a parachute.

As we said earlier, winners always try to accomplish at least two things at once.

A WIN A DAY

Taking control of your body and your appearance is an ideal example of how to be a winner as the victories are many, and usually quantifiable. In fact, for the first few weeks or so – perhaps even longer – it should be possible to mark up at least *one win a day*.

A BOOK OF VICTORIES

It's worthwhile keeping a special diary, in addition to the complete record of your journey on the road to becoming a winner, in which to note down your victories on the way to fitness.

Write down on the first page your measurements, weight etc. and whether you want to increase or decrease your weight. If you take a fitness test before starting, make sure you get a copy of the results and enter them in your diary. You should also enter your performance details, for example, '3 minutes on exercise bike at low resistance, five sit ups, jogged 200 yards', and so on.

Unless you are already very fit you can almost guarantee that, looking back at your diary after a couple of weeks, your performance on the first day will seem pathetic but, for the moment, aim each day for an increase in the numbers of at least one of the exercises you do and don't forget that every improvement is a win. In many ways, the more unfit you are at the moment the more obvious will be the improvement. But don't forget – *take it easy and go for the glow.*

> **Tip from the Top**
>
> 'Winning is constantly improving everything.'

9

WINNERS DESERVE THE BEST

Winners deserve their rewards: every victory, however small, should be rewarded. As a winner, if you have people working for you, you will know how much rewards are appreciated, even if they are nothing more than a smile or a verbal pat on the back. Your own superiors, however, may not be quite so perceptive and, although in the long run you should be able to educate them by example, in the meantime, when you chalk up a victory, you should celebrate by rewarding yourself.

Even the smallest win is worth a small smile of self-congratulations and, while smirking is definitely a no-no, there is no earthly reason why you should not look cheerful if you have just proved yourself a winner. In fact, that's yet another of the admonitions from our schooldays that we can jettison at last. Remember your teachers roaring 'I'll teach you to look so pleased with yourself!' – meaning, of course, exactly the opposite. If only they had concentrated on making us pleased with ourselves, and even allowing us to show it, instead of accentuating the mediocre and preaching the joys of conformity. Years later, in the army and at work, clones of these depressing tyrants are still shouting 'You're not here to think!' or 'You're not here to enjoy yourselves!' to which even an apprentice winner replies – though perhaps *sotto voce* – 'Of course we bloody are!'

WINNERS ARE PLEASED WITH THEMSELVES – AND IT SHOWS

The great thing about being a winner is that you are pleased with yourself in the sense of the French phrase we use meaning 'happy in one's skin'. This, of course, has nothing to do with self-satisfaction which upsets people and is therefore counter-productive, but means simply that winners are pleased to be who they are, pleased to be doing what they are doing, happy to be winning and not particularly anxious to change places with anyone on earth. 'He wouldn't call the Queen his Aunt' is the Lancashire equivalent of the French expression and that's not a bad definition of what it means to be a winner either.

WINNERS DESERVE THE BEST

A quiet smile is a fine reward for those tiny victories winners experience all the time, but the win of the day, the win of the week or the *win of the month* deserves something a little more extravagant. Reward yourself for these with something positive and combine the rewards you give yourself with your winner's appreciation of excellence so that, in effect, you are – yet again – winning twice.

It needn't cost the earth. In fact, a win of the day could be celebrated at the cost of a few pence by changing your evening drink from, say, a pint of beer to a glass of malt whisky or fine wine.

ENJOY YOURSELF

There are two rewards to celebrate a win, both large and small, that have stood the test of time in all winning situations. You will always feel like a winner as you purchase either of them.

Flowers Fresh flowers are always appreciated and can be enjoyed by everybody at home and in the workplace. What is more, a gift of flowers shows real thoughtfulness on behalf of the giver, and like all the best 'winning awards' can often be shared by the recipient and many other people – including the donor.

Flowers can be sent quickly and efficiently at very low cost.

Champagne Celebrates a win more excitingly than any other drink.

When we say champagne, we don't necessarily mean expensive brands like Veuve Clicquot, Bollinger or Krug. We mean virtually any wine that sparkles and goes 'pop' when you take the wire off the cork, but celebrate according to your means, or just beyond.

Enjoy yourself!

FINE FEATHERS

Among those material possessions that tell others something about the sort of people we are, clothes rank very highly so it makes sense to reward ourselves for a reasonably important win by buying an item of clothing. It has no need to be a Savile Row suit, although there's a great deal of winning mileage to be had out of a really good 'whistle', but it should be the best you can afford of its kind.

Be extravagant in small things. It's useful to remember that the ideal present is something, however small, which is so extravagant that you wouldn't normally dream of buying it for yourself. In the case of a winner buying a reward, this is exactly what you do buy yourself. Not only does the reward make you feel good, and therefore more of a winner, but the raw silk tie or the hand-made shoes will lift whatever else you happen to be wearing into the winning bracket.

Incidentally, a minor win when buying the best is that it can turn out to be an economy – anyway, that's our story and we are sticking to it. Seriously though, if you are prepared to devote some time to looking after them it's often worth buying something like an expensive classic jacket or sports coat which will last for years and can't therefore be classed as extravagant.

WINNERS' TRADEMARKS

If it's something to wear, or to carry with you, your reward could become a trademark. A bow tie, for instance, has been used by several winning personalities to help them stand out from the crowd by giving them instant recognition. The same effect can be achieved by, say, an unusual watch, earrings or cuff-links. Women can usually teach the men in this respect, just as young people can show older people a thing or two.

Mind you, it's not too surprising that the older generation aren't exactly a bunch of sartorial extroverts with teachers like the one who told one woman we know, when she was a schoolgirl, 'Just let me catch any of you girls expressing yourselves here!'

Another useful reward item which could become a trademark is a really good fountain pen and ball-point set, especially if you work in an office where they are always in use and always in evidence. In this connection it is worth remembering that *winners are generous* and should appear so even in small things – come to think of it especially in small things. So use, for instance, a pen with a broad bold nib for signing your letters and practise a powerful 'winning' signature, especially if sending out letters under your name is part of your job.

BE GENEROUS WITH SPACE

Be generous with stationery, whether you are writing letters for your firm or for yourself. This doesn't mean you have to make paper aeroplanes out of the stuff, but it does mean allowing generous margins and spacing and a signature big enough to show you mean business.

Letter writing is an important way of selling yourself as a winner and one which costs nothing but a little thought. Try to send out all letters, especially business letters, without mistakes, but whatever you do, don't send scrunched up, mean looking letters with apologetic signatures.

MAKE AN EXHIBITION OF YOURSELF

Another piece of schoolday advice winners can do without is 'Don't make an exhibition of yourself' because, unless you can afford to pay a high priced PR man to do the job for you, you have to make an exhibition of yourself if you are going to be a winner.

Of course, there is a lot of difference between making an exhibition of one's self in the sense we mean and behaving like a total idiot. But while a great deal depends on the individual's personality, the only place where you are likely to win by appearing to be a total non-entity is aboard a hijacked aircraft.

In most other cases, getting yourself *favourably* noticed is a winning move. You have to sell yourself to be a winner and you should be your own best Public Relations Consultant.

PRACTICAL WINNING

Imagine that you are a top executive of a multinational PR company, who has just been given *you* as a client. The aim is to get your client noticed and to present him as a winner. You should try a couple of proposals, one for a limited budget and one where you can spend a little more money. Try to think up one or more down-to-earth schemes but, at the same time, try to come up with something really off-beat. Let your subconscious work for you on this one. You could easily come up with a winner.

We know one chap, for instance, who went out one day and bought himself an elderly Lagonda, in the days when such things were merely expensive rather than prohibitive, and found he had acquired an instant 'trademark' which was a genuine winner.

SHARE YOUR WINS – AND THE REWARDS

There's a lot of truth in the old saying about a trouble shared being a trouble halved. We all need a shoulder to cry on at times and most of us who have partners use them as sounding boards when we want to have a good moan. That's fine as long as it's not overdone and as long as there's a two-way traffic in damp shoulders. But for winners it is much more important to remember that *a win shared is a win doubled.*

When the homecomer answers the time-honoured question 'What sort of a day did you have?' with 'Pretty good actually. In fact I picked up a bottle of decent plonk to celebrate. If you like I'll tell you about it while we have a glass or two' the win is shared, celebrated *and reinforced* all at the same time. It also makes for a much better atmosphere than a non-commital growl and, as allowing someone into a part of your life they don't always share completely is something of an intimacy reinforcer, this makes for yet another win.

Share your wins in the workplace too, especially if colleagues have contributed towards the victory. It needn't be anything big – a box of chocolates or a bottle of wine, for example, is hardly going to break you as a way of saying 'thank you' to the team that helped you achieve great sales figures or whatever, but it counts a hell of a lot more than the thought and in some cases more than money.

It is pleasant to give a tangible reward, whether to ourselves or to others, but they don't have to be expensive and in the case of QED, for example – the industrial motivation scheme – one of the incentives offered is a simple coffee mug and another is a pen in a presentation box.

When you are rewarding yourself though for a really big win, think of something you have always wanted and, if

A win shared is a win doubled

you can reasonably (or even unreasonably) afford it, *treat yourself*. It could be anything from a new hairdo to a world cruise, with lots of scope in between, from a new car to a visit to a health farm.

Make a list of the rewards you would like to give yourself for wins, ranging from the smallest to the biggest you can think of. Remember that winners, while they do try to put something by for a rainy day, are rarely miserly or anxious to make a good showing in the 'Recent Wills' column of their local paper.

PRACTICAL WINNING

List of Treats

Holiday
Weekend at Health Farm
New Car
New Clothes
Watch
Jewellery
Furniture

Your List

....

....

....

....

....

....

There's a nasty puritanical streak about those people who are convinced that there is something fundamentally wrong about enjoying the rewards of winning, whatever they may be, and that spending the money you have earned on the good things of life is especially wicked.

We firmly believe that this is total rubbish and that, once you have taken care of things like food and housing for yourself and your dependants, and perhaps sent a few bob to those who have little chance to win, you should concentrate on the things you enjoy. Whatever your favourite cliché relating to the taboo subject of d-e-a-t-h, it really is true that 'we pass this way but once' and 'in the midst of life' etc., and, no matter what the old time schoolmasters and the rest used to tell us, we winners *are* here to enjoy ourselves in the workplace, in the home, the pub, the concert hall, the country, the theatre – in fact everywhere.

WINNERS AREN'T PENNY PINCHERS

Winners tend not to pinch pennies and in fact will always travel *first class*, both literally and metaphorically, if they can afford it, and sometimes even when they really can't.

A winner travelling by train for an interview, say, will find the extra few quid for a First Class ticket because it makes him feel like a winner all the way. On the way back he'll probably stop off to pick up a little something as a reward for at least doing his best, whatever the outcome.

> ### Tip from the Top
>
> 'Little things do mean a lot.'

10

WIN WITH A WINNING TEAM

Once you know what to look for it's pretty easy to spot winners as people who are poised, confident, fit-looking and above all, happy, as we put it, 'in their skin'. In fact, they might just as well be wearing badges proclaiming their winning status, but what is particularly striking is that almost all of them seem to be members of a winning team.

There are some winners who are loners but, if so, it is always from choice and if they are, for example, freelances in the workplace they will usually be found to be working for winning clients, perhaps in addition to being members of a winning team on the leisure front. For the most part winners are to be found in winning teams and it should not come as a shock for us to learn that this is not a coincidence. Of course, winners do *create* winning teams and this is a very important part of being a winner. But often, especially in the workplace, a much easier way is to join a winning team.

FINDING A WINNING TEAM

Before you can join a winning team you have to find one. Curiously enough, identifying a winning team is as easy to do, and as difficult to define, as identifying and defining an individual winner. Winning groups do share many of the characteristics of the winning individuals we have been looking at.

Naturally, not all the winning teams we are considering wear jerseys. At first sight some of them may not even look like teams at all because the winning teams we mean range from small offices to multi-national industries and from infantry sections to vast armies. However, since the principles involved are much the same for all groups it will be helpful to look first at teams that *do* wear jerseys and you could begin by making a list of some of the sporting teams past and present that have been genuine winners.

You could then list some of their characteristics; for example:

(1) Winning teams have a great many winners in them; most of the players are poised, confident, etc. and although they may well be 'stars' in their own right they are confident enough to allow others to shine and to help them to be winners.

(2) Winning teams have the winning habit and because they usually have more winning games behind them than otherwise they go into every game expecting to win.

(3) Winning teams often include winning groups and combinations, like a winning forward line or a winning defence, which work together so well they sometimes seem to have a sixth sense, whereas in fact they have merely learned to co-operate to make each other winners and to make the team a winning team.

(4) Winning teams develop a special energy that comes from winning and which increases not by simple progression but geometrically, which means that a group of, say, four winners doesn't have the winning energy

of four individual winners but a great deal more. (This is called synergy.)

(5) A winning team develops both mental and physical energy. It can withstand adversity better than a losing team, coming back for more when defeat seems almost inevitable – not to mention doing a strenuous lap of honour when victory is finally achieved.

(6) Winning teams create a winning atmosphere. Their winning aura may even surround the 'losing' team so that all the spectators go away happy – as winners – and the losing team shares in the glamour of 'a match to remember', having raised their game to the best of which they are capable. Everyone, in fact, emerges a winner.

(7) With a winning team, winning is contagious so that newcomers soon acquire the team's magic – *but* they do have to be playing in the right league.

Of course, all sorts of forces tend to ensure that football players, soldiers, executives and the rest of us do not play out of our leagues and it should happen less often to a winner than others.

However, should you find yourself playing in the wrong league – for whatever reason – move!!

This applies particularly in the workplace where sociologists have identified the Peter Principle, or a tendency to promote people to positions just beyond their capabilities, which is a total NO WIN situation, both for the individual and the team concerned. The first remedy is to move to another department or even another firm and then perhaps to consider the possibilities like retraining, additional experience and so on.

Remember . . . a winner can win in any league – except the wrong one.

JOINING A WINNING TEAM – IN THE WORKPLACE

As we have seen there are winning teams in every league and, as even winners have to begin somewhere, it is as well, especially in the working context, to join a winning team. Later, for the experienced winner, for whom winning has become a habit, there will be advantages – and a great deal of satisfaction – to be gained by joining a team which has winning potential and turning it round. But for the moment let's think about joining a ready-made winning team.

To do this we need to know what sort of organisation we intend joining. Even when jobs are hard to come by, it is worthwhile making a few inquiries about the state of industrial relations in our proposed workplace.

AGGRO IS FOR LOSERS

Winners aren't doormats – precisely the opposite – but they don't go looking for a fight, so it's well worthwhile having a chat with someone who already works in your intended workplace, preferably in a similar job to the one you are after or even in the same department. Very often newspapers and libraries can be useful sources of information as to whether or not the organisation you intend joining is a winner.

A history of industrial disputes, for example, especially

over trivial matters, might make you think twice, while glowing tributes at retirement parties combined with lots of success stories would be encouraging. One legacy of the Industrial Revolution we can well do without is the division of employers and employees, management and workforce, foremen and workers and skilled and unskilled into any of the multifarious versions of 'them' and 'us'.

Of course, in the bad old days there was often plenty of reason for the workers to act against selfish, ruthless bosses. But while human nature hasn't changed much, if at all, the climate certainly has and, in most cases, enlightened self-interest is more likely to control the actions of both workers and management than historical antagonisms. Today, most employers and employees realise that in many ways what is good for one is good for the other; and if they don't there are usually, though not always, enough checks and balances to ensure that they at least respect each other's position.

This only means that most firms have moved nearer to a winning stance than their predecessors of the 'trouble at t'mill' days. But winners want much more than that and a firm that intends to win is going to have to provide it. For the genuine winner in the workplace, winning is not a question of putting one over on either colleagues or management. In the same way, in a winning organisation, whether it is a tiny office or a multinational concern, winning, for management, is not a question of conning the individual into doing more work for less.

In fact, a winning organisation – like a winning individual – will attempt to do away with as much 'work' as possible by making employment enjoyable.

When we look at the sort of things which persuade us to

undertake any particular form of activity, we are talking about *motivation* and when the activity is in the workplace we are talking about *industrial motivation*. This has become a science but, if we look at some of the aspects of Industrial Motivation, we discover that we have already talked about many of the motivating factors in an informal way when we were considering how winners motivate themselves.

This sounds as though it could be bad for your eyes and only goes to show that a great deal of specialist jargon can be off-putting and self-defeating. So let's instead ask what – especially in the workplace – are the sort of things that are liable to get us, and the people who work with us, for us, or under us, up off our butts.

WHAT MAKES JOHNNY RUN? – IT'S NOT JUST MONEY BY A LONG CHALK

Make no mistake, most winners like money and the things money can buy as much as anyone, but Industrial Motivation experts identify no less than sixteen non-financial motivating factors. These include:

(1) **FEAR**

In the bad old days, fear was often the physical fear of being hurt. There were any number of physical punishments, from flogging to torture and even execution. Fortunately, in modern times, the physical fear does not apply. Instead, we have many mental fears of which, curiously enough, one of the main ones is the fear of doing the wrong thing. There is also the fear of making a fool of ourselves and the fear of getting caught if we know we have done wrong.

Fear is more a manipulative factor than a motivating factor, but it is so important that it must head any list of motivations. History has many examples of leaders using fear as their main weapon.

One fear that many people have is the fear of losing their job, and the fear of being poor.

Winners are less fearful than most people.

(2) **GREED**
We wouldn't be human if we didn't sometimes want a little bit more. Usually, we are too embarrassed to display greed publicly, but in ourselves we usually want that little bit extra – the biggest piece of cake, a larger house, and of course more money.

Winners are only human in this respect but they don't allow greed to rule their lives.

(3) **COMPETITION**
Most people are highly competitive. A small number of people are so competitive that they always want to be top or the best. The majority of people, however, are in a smaller category and, while they are not prepared to go to extremes to be absolutely at the top, nevertheless do not want to be beaten by their peers or anyone they consider inferior. Competition not to be bottom of the league is often more powerful than competition to reach the top. Realistically, many people are content to be in the middle, but if their rankings start to drop they will immediately become more competitive.

Winners enjoy competitions they can win. They can be serious, but rarely deadly serious, about competition and tend to appreciate its 'game play' aspect.

(4) **RECOGNITION**
This is a posh word for saying 'thank you'. 'It costs nothing

to be polite'. Saying 'thank you' is good manners and is always appreciated. Adults, just like children and animals, like to be thanked frequently. There is a tendency to believe that saying 'thank you' is demeaning, but this is simply not true. It makes both the giver and the receiver feel good.

Manners maketh winners.

(5) **PRIDE**

Be proud of what you do and who you do it for. It is no good being apologetic and ashamed of your occupation. Every single person in every organisation, however large, is important. However lowly you may think you are, you are nevertheless playing a vital role. We do not know of anyone who is intentionally paid for doing nothing. Military people of all nations are experts in the use of pride as a motivation factor; so much so that they can sometimes persuade people to die for it.

Winners walk tall and, as they used to say in the army, with 'bags of swank'.

(6) **INVOLVEMENT**

Getting involved is very motivating, but sometimes people don't know how to start. The best way to get involved, and to show that you want to get involved, is to ask questions. Asking questions shows that you are taking an interest as well as getting involved.

Another way of getting involved is to constantly look at ways of improving what you are doing and the environment in which you work. Very small ideas for change are a form of involvement. Be prepared to challenge statements like 'We've always done it that way'. Involvement is one of the key areas in which you can enjoy your work more and it is easy to get started.

Winners ask questions to learn – and question assumptions to live.

(7) **BELONGING**

It is very motivating to feel part of a winning team, club, village, or any identifiable group. British people are very keen on joining clubs and the feeling of belonging is very strong.

The opposite to belonging is being 'left out', which is not always very comfortable.

Winners enjoy belonging and as they tend to be good company are usually sought after.

(8) **STATUS**

British people are still very class conscious, which means they are status conscious too. Again, military people are great experts in status, only they call it by a different name, rank. They are also very clever to give each rank a different uniform or badge. Status in civilian life is much more subtle, but nevertheless is extremely important. Job titles in effect define a form of status and therefore should be as descriptive and as positive as possible. Status symbols are a clever commercial exploitation of this motivation factor.

Winners usually enjoy status, and even status symbols, as much as anyone but they don't *need* them in order to be identified as winners.

(9) **FUN**

Smiling and enjoying ourselves is actually healthy! Why shouldn't we enjoy our lives more? In fact, the whole of this book is intended to emphasise this point. Make it a habit to smile more and you will find it is infectious and people invariably smile back. It is just as easy to develop the habit to smile as it is to scowl, so be positive and enjoy yourself.

Winners enjoy life.

(10) **CHALLENGE**
Big challenges can be intimidating, but small challenges can be motivating. The small challenges often begin with the phrase 'Bet you can't!' Bet you can't finish this by Friday is a challenge that many people can't resist. It also stirs the competitive spirit. However, if the challenge is too great then it will not be taken up and this will be demotivating. Look for the small challenges and each challenge achieved is a minor win.

Winners begin by challenging themselves.

(11) **ADVENTURE**
A new experience is an adventure. All change can be treated as an adventure. We look for adventure as part of our holidays so why shouldn't we look for adventure at work. By calling a new task an adventure you can catch people's imagination and get their co-operation as well.

For the winner, all life is an adventure, whether it involves the body or the mind.

(12) **HELPING OTHERS**
Helping others less fortunate than ourselves can be very motivating. Contributing to charity is an obvious way to help others, and it is amazing how motivating some fund-raising is. Sponsored swims, sponsored walks, sponsored runs are an everyday occurrence and are enjoyed by many.

Winners are no slouches when it comes to charity and good works but have also been known to help people *more* fortunate than themselves.

THE FINAL FOUR

Leadership

The word 'leader' is an intimidating one and builds the picture of a great leader like Churchill or Napoleon. In fact, most of the world is run by 'little' leaders and the definition of a leader is simply 'the person in charge'. In business, the leader is called a manager, a supervisor, a chargehand, etc. etc. Every team or group of people must have somebody in charge and that person is the leader. The most effective team size is ten or eleven people or even smaller. The Roman army, for example, had sections of ten, and most sports have teams of eleven, of whom one is a playing leader or captain.

In the workplace, the leader usually has managerial duties in addition to other duties, but this is not essential. The leader may, in fact, be doing an identical job to his team mates exactly as in many sports. However, it is essential that every member of the team knows who the leader is as the lack of a clear system is very demotivating and leads to chaos.

Winners are often those people others look to for leadership, especially in times of crisis.

Plan

Every team has a plan and the leader is in charge of the plan. No one plans to fail, but many fail to plan. There must be a plan whether it is a five-year plan, a one-year plan, a one-month plan, a one-week plan, a one-day plan, a one-morning, a one-hour plan or a one-minute plan etc. Without proper planning nothing will work effectively. Ideally, plans should be written down and shared wherever possible. Ownership of the plan by the team is one of the essential ingredients for winning.

Winners plan to win.

Deadlines

If you have forever to do something, that is exactly how long it will take. All plans must have a deadline, and this deadline should be practical and visible. Deadlines are very motivating as everybody hates to miss a deadline. Missing a deadline is losing, and beating a deadline is winning.

Winners arrange to meet their deadlines – without actually panting.

Achievement

Achievement is the satisfaction of finishing the job. On time! It can be the satisfaction of crossing off the task from your list. It is the most motivating of all the factors because it can be summed up in one word. Winning!

Tip from the Top

'Show me a good loser and I'll show you a loser.'

11

WINNERS LIKE TO SAY 'YES'

Winners like to say 'yes' because it makes the other person feel like a winner and helps spread the winning feeling throughout the home or the workplace. They know that saying 'yes' to another person's request can be a subtle form of 'stroking' because, whether they are being asked for the loan of a pencil or a hefty rise, the decision-making process is an exercise of power.

Because they are aware of this – either consciously or subconsciously – winners prefer to say 'yes' graciously, or at least not grudgingly. Their decision in some cases may be the same as that of the non-winner but whereas the non-winner will make it obvious that a favour is being granted reluctantly, the winner will make it plain that the favour, once decided on, has been granted willingly.

Of course, there are times when even winners can't be expected to make on-the-spot decisions. But these won't usually be questions of whether or not to lend a pencil or any other relatively trivial matter and even in such cases the winner will normally explain why a decision can't be made at once and, more importantly, say exactly when a decision can be expected.

DECISIONS

In most day-to-day exchanges, however, the winner will have the confidence to make an immediate decision and will not only do his best to say 'yes' but will use the opportunity to make the other person feel even more of a winner by using words like 'certainly', 'glad to be of help' or 'let's give it a go'.

DIFFICULT DECISIONS

Naturally, in the real world, not all requests can be granted immediately, or even granted at all, but there is a tremendous difference between a 'That's a tough one but we'll see what we can do' and a non-negotiable 'Can't be done'.

Winners are quite capable of pointing out how difficult it may be to fulfil any given request, but they won't make it out to be more difficult than it is, and if things are going to take some time they will normally explain why this is the case. They will also try, wherever possible, to give the explanations themselves, especially when the decision is an important one, because otherwise their decisions could be misinterpreted and their motives misunderstood.

SEND THREE AND FOURPENCE – WE'RE GOING TO A DANCE

There's an old World War Two story about some soldiers in the Western Desert who passed back a message by word of mouth – 'Send reinforcements, we're going to advance'.

When it eventually reached Headquarters it had changed into 'Send three and fourpence, we're going to a dance'. In real life it is more likely to be the tone of the message that is altered than the content so that, for example, a polite request reaches its recipient as a curt, imperious summons which is totally self-defeating.

Winners are normally good at communicating insofar as they speak clearly and distinctly with a pleasant easy manner because they know that getting their message across is important. When they can, they deliver the message themselves.

SHAME THE DEVIL

Winners, as we've already made clear, are not candidates for sainthood, but they do tend to tell the truth, if only out of self-interest, because the truth is easier to remember and it is embarrassingly non-winner to be caught out in a lie.

Naturally, winners are no strangers to the face-saving white lie, especially if the face they are saving belongs to someone else. But they also know that truth is bankable and that a reputation for complete truthfulness can come in very handy on those rare occasions when they are forced to be less than candid.

INTRODUCING THE JOBSWORTHS

If Mr and Mrs Winner and all the little Winners are among the top players in the game of life then the Jobsworth family are definitely pretty close to the bottom. However, they do have one important function for the intending winner in that they are the perfect example of how *not* to do things.

We've all met them of course. A great many of the male members of the Jobsworth family, for instance, seem to find occupations which place them in cages – not, unfortunately, zoo type cages but the sort from which they can peer out onto the rest of the world and utter the mournful, distinctive cry of the species ''Smore than me job's worth'. Other male Jobsworths graduate to positions of authority like foremen, ticket inspectors, minor civil servants and the like but only the accent changes as they intone 'I'm afraid it's more than my job's worth'.

Female Jobsworths can hold all the above jobs but, in addition, are to be found in shops, stores and other places where they can inflict themselves on the general public. Meanwhile, the smaller Jobsworths are busily picking up the family habits, changing from objectionable children who know no other words than 'Can't', 'Shan't' and 'Won't' into even more despicable teenagers who are already looking for jobs in which their talent for saying 'No' can be exploited to the full. They are also presumably working on the thumbs down techniques they will need in future when they exclaim 'Can't be done Mate' or 'Absolutely out of the question, I'm afraid', followed by the ritual ''Smore than me job's worth'.

JOBSWORTHS NEVER WIN

Of course the one, and occasionally the only, consoling thing about the Jobsworth tribe is that the jobs, to the worth of which they refer so frequently, are rarely worth very much at all.

Mr and Mrs Jobsworth

Jobsworths may think they are winning when they intone their magic phrase and insist on going by the book or their own whim to deliver their totally non-negotiable 'No!' But even though a few unenlightened managers may promote them to positions of cannon fodder executives, whose functions are to take all the flak from below, they will very rarely achieve really important positions and will certainly never become winners.

WINNERS IN A JOBSWORTH'S JOB

Jobsworths can't win but a winner in what might be thought of as a typically Jobsworth job can work wonders. Sometimes they can turn the whole department or the whole factory into winners and win promotions for themselves – if they want it. These are the sort of commissionaires who say 'Hang on, I'll find him for you', the storekeepers who say 'Let me have a look' and the receptionists who say 'I'll see what I can do'.

Like the commissionaire we know who made his job into a small department and his department into one of the most efficient, smoothest running and well liked in Fleet Street, they are winners who like to say 'yes', who make other people feel like winners for the rest of the day and who, above all, are 'happy in their skin'.

WINNERS VERSUS JOBSWORTH

Of course winners are just as likely to come up against the various members of the Jobsworth clan as anyone else but they do seem to have less trouble with them than most other people. This is partly because Jobsworths can usually spot a winner and have well honed survival instincts which make them anxious to please but mainly because winners habitually use *winning assumptions.*

WINNING ASSUMPTIONS

Making winning assumptions is a technique which comes

so naturally to winners as to be almost second nature, so much so that many of them use it all the time without being aware that they are doing so. Its function goes far beyond dealing with the infuriating Jobsworth clan but its use in that context makes an interesting example.

A winning assumption consists, quite simply, of taking it for granted that the person you are talking to will be happy to do as you ask. For example, a winner confronted by a Jobsworth commissionaire or receptionist would not say 'I wonder if I could possibly have a word with Mr Quickstempel,' but something like 'Good Morning. My name is Winner, Total Winner and I'm here to see Mr Algernon Quickstempel. Would you be kind enough to tell him I'm here'. In fact the assumption lies as much in the tone of voice as in what is said, the tone in this case being friendly but firm and totally confident, without appearing in the least hectoring. In this case, without being much more than reasonably well mannered, the winner has made Jobsworth feel a little bit more human than usual by wishing him a cheery good morning, established himself as a person whose name is of importance, stated his business in a positive manner and conveyed a hint that he may possibly be on first name terms with Mr. Quickstempel. At the same time he has suggested a course of action to Jobsworth – many of whose family are ditherers – in a way which makes it difficult to refuse.

LICENCED JOBSWORTHS

Some Jobsworths are appointed as flak takers or guardians precisely because of their otherwise losing traits. They will not rise higher but they get a charge out of saying 'no' and are the sort of people who would not let you in to see their boss if you were delivering a Football Pools cheque. Making these individuals feel human is quite a trick, but one which winners often pull off, especially if there is repeated contact. Winners know that *a Jobsworth who becomes a 'mate' is a valuable contact.* Winners do this by making the Jobsworth in question feel like a winner in the same way that they make everyone with whom they come into contact feel more of a winner than before.

LET'S ASSUME

Using your tape recorder try out a few different approaches to a typical Jobsworth, a commissionaire for example, or a private secretary whose boss you wish to see on important business, or a storekeeper who won't even tell you if he has a part in stock without complete documentation in six languages and a personal request from the Managing Director.

Try first an approach which does not embody a winning assumption. Then make the same request while assuming that Mr, Mrs or Miss Jobsworth is going to find agreeing to it the most natural thing in the world. Jobsworths are often found in shops and in non-winning restaurants so you could try one of these service situations first if you find it easier, before tackling a Jobsworth whose 'non-negotiable No!' is backed by some sort of official position – however lowly.

BEWARE OF THE PSEUDO-WINNER

Winning assumptions are so effective that winners who use

them effortlessly have to be careful to avoid exploiting not only the people who work with them, but their own friends and families as well. The danger is that the power, and it is a power, to persuade people to do as one wishes is habit forming – for both parties – and it's very easy to misuse it without even being aware that one is doing so. In extreme cases this can result in a master-slave relationship which no real winner would allow to develop.

However, there are people around who are only too happy to abuse the habit forming aspect of the winning assumption. They are usually people who have read the sort of books on Man Management which come with their own chair and whip. Their method is to use winning assumptions to gain, not a rapport, but dominance. They are often to be found in the workplace where they tend to practise this form of manipulation on people of equal or slightly lower rank to themselves.

At first their operations seem fairly innocuous, beginning perhaps with requests to fetch them something from one end of the office to the other because they are busy typing or talking on the phone, or to deliver a message in another part of the building as it's 'on your way'. Should you find yourself in this situation, all seems perfectly harmless at first but, over a period of time, you could find yourself virtually working for your demanding 'friend' who could then even succeed in having his 'obviously' dominant position ratified by your mutual boss.

Winners are especially easily put upon in this respect as one of their winning assumptions is that everyone likes them and besides, they are not normally suspicious. However, they will usually realise what is happening before it's too late, which is just as well because a striking feature of this particular dominance ploy is that it is virtually impossible to operate if the intended victim is aware of what is going on. Winners will use one of their big guns – humour – against such operators, without even having to refuse his minor requests. For example, the attempt to make the intended victim into an 'obvious' messenger recoils when the recipient is told with a grin 'that idle blighter Smartarse asked me to drop these off'.

The difference between the pseudo-winner who deliberately sets out to dominate, and the real winner who has everyone from the office cleaner to the Managing Director doing him favours, is one of the nuances of the winning game and can be seen clearly only in the light of the way other people react.

Winners never leave people feeling that they have been conned – except in the nicest possible way.

MORE WINNING IN THE WORKPLACE

Winners are positive people and a winner will make a decision one way or another if it is in his or her province to do so, doing their best to be of assistance and apologising if they really can't help out. Often, if they can't do anything themselves, they will refer the matter to someone who can. If they don't know the answer to a query, for example, they do know where they can find out and are usually willing to do so.

Winners, in fact, get as much of a charge, or more, out of saying 'yes' as the Jobsworths get out of saying 'no'. They are pleasantly assertive because they can afford to be, mainly because they are good at their jobs which they find challenging enough to be interesting without being stress-making. As we've mentioned, they would normally feel happy to tackle a job senior to their own but, for the moment, they are thoroughly enjoying what they are doing. Being good at one's job and enjoying the use of one's expertise is, as the experts are fond of saying, 'highly motivational'.

THE WINNER IN THE WORKPLACE LITMUS TEST

Ask yourself how many times a year you get up and say 'Oh God! Not another bloody Monday!' If it's more than three – after all, even winners get the blues every now and then – you are not winning in the workplace. Remember, winners have given up 'work' as much as possible in favour of interesting and enjoyable employment.

Most jobs can be made enjoyable but not if you find them stressful. Don't be afraid to ask for help or advice if there is an aspect of the job you're not happy about. It shows a fundamental confidence and is a thousand times better than trying to fudge things.

If you *are* doing a job you do well and enjoy, you are a winner. Otherwise, even if you are the boss, you are most certainly a loser and should think about a sideways move or perhaps a change of job.

WINNERS CAN SAY 'NO'!

Winners like to say 'yes' but this doesn't mean they are pushovers and they can say 'no' if they have to. However, they do so pleasantly. We know of one major company who employed a professional letter writer especially to write 'difficult' letters. He was reputed to be so good that he could write a letter of dismissal which made the recipient feel great about getting the sack.

Using the tape recorder, try your hand at saying 'no' to several different requests while making the other person feel a winner. Then write a couple of letters of dismissal, one beginning, say, 'This is to notify you . . .' and the other on the lines of 'Dear Bill, I have felt for some time now that you have not been completely happy here at Bloggs Brothers and, although we shall be sorry to see you go . . .'.

WINNERS ARE FRIENDLY

Being cheerful and friendly makes all the difference in your relationships with others because being friendly shows that you *care*. You *care* about the person you are talking to, you *care* about his problems and you *care* about helping him to solve these problems.

Some organisations train their employees in improving the quality of Customer Care and this type of people training is becoming increasingly important. It is also becoming increasingly specialised. But if you want to sum up the technical jargon relating to this change of attitude in one word, then that word is 'friendliness'. It shows that you care for people and therefore care for your customers.

Sales people talk to the actual customer. But the secret is to get all employees thinking of their colleague as a customer, the next department as a customer and so on. The benefit is a more friendly organisation, a more winning organisation and of course it is the real customers who pay our salaries.

There is a short term risk that if you are too friendly

non-winners will take advantage of you so you have to learn to spot this situation when it occurs. Non-winning bosses of the autocratic type sometimes mistake friendliness for weakness. But even autocrats can be winners and it may be useful to ask yourself 'Is he a just bastard – or is he just a bastard?'

Winners will always win in the long run. Being a winner means that, not only do you *not* behave like a bastard, you don't even have to feel like a bastard . . . and that's only one of the advantages of being a winner, as we shall see when we look into the *payoff*, the sixty-four-thousand-dollar question of *what's in it for me?*

Tip from the Top

'A CUSTOMER'

Is the most important person in any business

Is not dependent on us – we depend on him

Is not someone to argue or match wits with

A customer deserves the best treatment you give him because it is *his* money that pays *your* salary.

12

WHAT'S IN IT FOR ME?

Okay – so you've decided to become a winner, or perhaps more of a winner than you already are. You've made up your mind to try at least some of the things we've suggested so far, both in the workplace and away from it, mainly because everyone likes to see themselves as poised and confident and it's intriguing to think that you can *train* yourself to be a winner. However, at the same time, you are almost certainly asking yourself, 'What's the bottom line? It's all very well asking us to do all these things, to behave in this way, to speak to people in such a way but, after all – what's in it for me?'

THE GLITTERING PRIZES

Well, as a winner, you will almost certainly be fitter, more attractive, happier and will live longer – which isn't bad for starters. You could also be more successful and make a lot of money. As we've pointed out, in the game of life there are more prizes than people, and winning can become a habit.

Fitter? Well, we've already talked about becoming fitter but being a winner brings its own fitness bonuses because, as a winner, you are less likely to be stressed, less likely to suffer from heart disease, to become an alcoholic or smoke too much. Winning also gives you tremendous energy – watch the winning team run a lap of honour while the losers collapse exhausted – so you feel fitter all the time. Again, there are those captains of industry, some of them quite elderly, who have a reputation for tireless energy and tackle a punishing work schedule that leaves their younger executives running to keep up. Their secret is that they aren't really working – they are winners who are thoroughly enjoying themselves.

As a winner, say the safety experts, you are also less likely than other people to have an accident either in the workplace or elsewhere, which could also add to your life span.

ALL IT TAKES IS A SMILE

As we've mentioned, winners do tend to smile a great deal and according to the British Safety Council smiling and laughter can reduce accidents, help performance at work and add years to your life. According to the Council's Director General, James Tye, smiling will help you to lead a happier, stress-free life. 'All it takes is a smile' he says, 'and you are on your way to feeling better and looking healthier'. We say smile and you're on your way to becoming a winner.

Happier? Well, winning is enjoyable so you will certainly be happier as a winner. As a winner you'll look forward to going to work as an opportunity to demonstrate your skills or expertise, perhaps to earn praise and to increase your self-esteem. You'll also enjoy meeting your colleagues and fellow winners, fellow members of a winning team. We remember one particular organisation whose employees worked incredibly hard for murderously long hours without the slighest complaint, mainly because what they would have been amused to hear referred to as their 'working environment' was that of a rather good club whose members were almost surprised to be paid for having such a stimulating and enjoyable time.

WINNING GIVES US BACK HALF OUR LIVES

Feeling good about going to work is a major win because we spend approximately a third of our lives at work, plus more hours getting to and from work and, frequently, more hours thinking about work in our 'spare' time.

Losers try to switch off when they set off for work and remain switched off, or at least put their brains on automatic until they get home again. They certainly don't enjoy the intervening period; often they actually hate it, which means they are wasting their lives. This is why *winning at work gives us back half of our waking lives.*

WINNERS ARE MORE ATTRACTIVE?

It sounds a bit like an ad. 'Be more attractive to your colleagues, to the boss, to the opposite sex!' but, in fact, winners *are* more attractive people than losers. Would you rather spend time with a happy winner or a miserable grouch of a loser?

Certainly winners tend to be more attractive to the opposite sex than losers and, even if some losers collect the sympathy vote, it is rarely the basis of a good relationship. Winners know that in a relationship or a family situation, in order to win themselves, they have to be part of a winning couple or a winning family. They don't feel, for example, that marriage is a battle which one party has to lose.

WINNERS HAVE A BETTER SEX LIFE?

Certainly. Sex, in fact, is a perfect example of non-competitive winning in which you become a winner by making sure that the other person wins, thus creating a winning partnership. Married winners extend this winning partnership to cover all aspects of their lives and are frequently described by other people as 'lucky' but, while they are certainly fortunate, luck as such doesn't necessarily have much to do with it. It is simply that the winner's confidence and self-esteem means they don't feel the need to dominate their partners and a genuine shared relationship becomes possible, giving winners a good chance of a happy marriage and, best of all, of a happy, well-adjusted family with kids who pick up winning habits from the outset. In other words, a marriage – like a person – can be 'happy in its skin'.

WINNERS ARE RICHER AND MORE SUCCESSFUL?

At last, the nitty gritty, the bottom line, the nub, the pith, the essence. After all, it's all very well talking about motivation but what about the money?

Well, winners do tend to be at the very least comfortable in the financial sense – although, for short periods at least, and especially if they know the situation to be only temporary, they can manage with less than other people. Being broke can be a challenge to a winner, provided he or she knows that help is available if needed. Jeffrey Archer, for example, lost a fortune and was hundreds of thousands of pounds in debt but came back to make a second fortune by writing books.

However, Archer didn't lose his decent suits, his education or his friends and presumably was not in much doubt as to where his next meal was coming from. Being permanently unemployed, and hopelessly so – which is, we suppose, the nearest one can get to real poverty in this country without opting out of the system – is very different, but here again winners have built-in resources which nobody can take away from them.

On one housing estate in Glasgow virtually everyone was unemployed until recently. Most of them, understandably, had sunk into complete apathy and depression but one man had spent his time doing up his house and garden and tending an allotment which supplied the family with all the fruit and vegetables they needed. He had also taken up watch repairing as a potentially remunerative hobby and was teaching himself French. In addition to all this, he was also spending a specific amount of time per week in an active search for a job and there seemed little doubt that of all the men on the estate he would be first to be employed. In the meantime, unemployed or not, he was a happy man – and a winner.

In the main, however, winners do succeed in the workplace – after all, who would you rather employ: a winner who could make the department, the office or the workshop a winner, or a loser who would infect his colleagues with his own loser's gloom? More to the point, who would you rather promote? It is the winner's power to inspire others to win as much as anything else which makes him a natural leader and in the workplace this brings rewards in terms of money and prestige.

WINNERS MAKE GOOD BOSSES

Real winners make splendid bosses and this is something that any Managing Director who is himself a winner will appreciate – which, of course, is one way in which winning permeates the whole organisation.

One reason they are such good bosses is that they allow every member of the team to make a contribution and acknowledge its importance. This doesn't mean that decisions are taken by committee. One officer we know of who commanded a small army unit had the right idea. He and his men gathered in the mess each evening to discuss the unit's task and everyone, even the most junior soldier present, was allowed to voice his ideas and criticisms over a drink. In the morning when the CO gave out his orders for the day the men could see that some of their ideas had been taken into account but, of course, at the morning meetings there was no discussion. The commanding officer would give his orders in the form of polite requests but there was no doubt that they were orders which had to be obeyed without question.

PERCEIVED WINNERS

One reason winners earn promotion and success in the workplace is that they are perceived to be winners. They have created a winning persona which is accepted by their colleagues, and their bosses and, where applicable, by the general public.

Sporting winners for instance become TV personalities, successful actors become politicians – even presidents – and politicians become successful authors, all because winners in one field are perceived as potential winners in other spheres. This is sometimes a little unfair on people who may be as well or better qualified than the chosen winners when it comes to the winners' secondary occupation – for example when sports stars get plum TV jobs. But it is a fact of life that winners get more chances to show what they are capable of than other people.

WINNERS GET MORE CHANCES

We've already pointed out that even winning at tiddleywinks will help you get the winning habit and that this will help you to become a winner elsewhere. But obviously if you are thinking of an outside win that will help make you a career winner you should try to make it more job related. An external degree or an Open University degree, for example, will be a useful demonstration of your winning abilities whatever discipline you choose. So if that's what you decide to do, pick a course that really interests you. Mastering job-related skills is another form of outside winning which could bring career success but, again, pick something that you want to do for the fun of it.

If you do a lot of driving in your job you could think about taking an advanced driving course as a source of satisfaction and, incidentally, as a talking point for your colleagues and bosses. Real winners aren't pushy but they are not anonymous either, especially in the workplace. If you work in a job where not all the people in a similar job to yourself are personally known to the individual who does the promoting, it is obvious that to be a career success – if that's what you have in mind – you need to be among those who *are* known, if only as the person who is learning Sanskrit or Origami.

Even if you make no special effort on the career front and are happy just to be a winner in the workplace and elsewhere, content to get as much enjoyment as possible out of doing the job well, you are going to stand out from the crowd and one way and another you will find it difficult to avoid promotion, success, money and the rest. Winners have these things thrust upon them.

SO – THAT'S IT THEN?

Well, you might be forgiven for thinking that when it comes to the 'What's in it for me?' bit, the foregoing is, as it were, it. After all, if becoming a winner can make you happier, fitter, more attractive, richer and more successful, not to mention helping you to live longer, it has to be well worth doing. In fact, however, there's a great deal more to it than that because winning is not only life extending but immensely life enhancing.

Taking charge of our lives, even if we only make a start by getting up a few minutes earlier than other people dictate, places us firmly among the 'doers' of this world.

WINNING IS LIFE ENHANCING

Remember the old joke about the man who went to the doctor and was given the sad news that he had not long to live? The doctor advised him to give up drinking, smoking, sex, music and television. 'Will that help me live longer?' he asked eagerly, to which the doctor replied 'I'm afraid not – but it will seem longer.' The point is that, while any sort of life is usually worth clinging on to, it is the quality of life that is really important, whether we measure the quality of our lives in terms of fine wine, country walks or great art – and winning improves the quality of life immensely.

One of the best examples of a winner we know is a woman who manages a family, has a successful career as a writer and in addition runs a luxury hotel renowned for its food. As a genuine winner, she is totally happy with her life, a great deal of the success of which is due to the fact that people like her. As a bonus she is able to choose as her guests the sort of people she describes as 'life enhancers', so that her house parties and dinners are gatherings of interesting and amusing winners. The fact that, in addition, she is being paid to do what she likes doing and does well puts her in a typical winner's situation.

WINNING IS MAGIC

'Give me Generals who are lucky' said Napoleon, meaning of course generals who were winners, generals who achieved victories with what seemed magic.

Nowadays, people say of winners that he or she has 'the magic touch' because they are the ones for whom everything seems to go not only right but splendidly and, in fact, there is a touch of magic about being a winner.

You can feel it every time you make a winning move –a pleasant tingle if the win is an everyday bit of winmanship or a great rush of euphoria if it's a biggie, better than booze and pretty nearly as good as sex. Like booze, it can induce everything from sheer contentment to a feeling of invincibility but, unlike booze, there's no hangover and both the feeling of content and the knowledge that you are likely to succeed in anything you undertake are real – and that's magic.

Best of all, of course, it's the sort of magic that can be acquired by almost anyone and we hope we've provided a few useful guidelines if not a magic wand.

So start winning *now*. It could well be the beginning of a winning streak that will last for the rest of your life.